Egbert W. Gillett

Gillett's Magic Cook Book

Egbert W. Gillett

Gillett's Magic Cook Book

ISBN/EAN: 9783744791830

Printed in Europe, USA, Canada, Australia, Japan

Cover: Foto ©Lupo / pixelio.de

More available books at **www.hansebooks.com**

GILLETT'S

Magic Cook Book

How to Obtain it:

BUY A PACKAGE OF MAGIC YEAST. IN IT YOU WILL FIND A RED TICKET. THE TICKET WILL TELL YOU HOW.

PUBLISHED BY
E. W. GILLETT, M'F'R MAGIC YEAST
CHICAGO, ILL.

INDEX

BREAD, BISCUITS, ROLLS, ETC.

Bread Making	137 to 142
French Bread	142
Brown Bread, (various kinds)	142-143
Corn Bread	144
Parker House Rolls	144
French Rolls	144-145
Biscuits	145-146
Hominy Fritters	147
Hominy Croquettes	147
Rice Fritters	147
Corn Fritters	147
Crumpets	148
Gems	148
Muffins	148-149
Pop-Overs	149
Waffles	150
English Buns	150
Rusks	151
Sally Lunn 1 and 2	151-152
French Twists	152
Rolls	152
Johnny Cakes	152
Raised Breakfast Cakes	153
Indian Meal Pancakes	153
Oat Meal Batter Cakes	153
Sour Milk Pancakes	154
Buckwheat Cakes	154
Bread Crumb Pancakes	154
Griddle Cakes	154
Green Corn Cakes	155
Flannel Cakes	155
Rice Cakes	155
Rye Gems	155
Rye Breakfast Cakes	156
Muffins	156
Spoon Corn Bread	157
Waffles	157
Breakfast Gems	158

BEVERAGES.

Chocolate	259
Rusian Tea	260
Lime Water	260
Sweet Whey	260
Grape Juice	260
Strawberry Wine	260
Milk Punch	261
Koumis or Sour Beer	261
Blackberry Cordial	261
Currant Wine	261
Raspberry Shrub	262
Arrowroot	262
Egg Nogg 1, 2 & 3	262
Egg Lemonade	263
Lemonade	263
Acid Lemonade	263
Lime-Ade	264
Orange-Ade	264
Tea and Coffee	364-265
To Roast Coffee	265

CROQUETTES

Croquettes	87 to 93

CAKES AND DOUGHNUTS

Watermelon Cake	209
Almond Cake	209
Almond Cream Cake	210
Chocolate Cream Cake	210-211
Chocolate Macaroons	212
Lemon Jelly Cake	212
Jelly Cake	212
Jelly Roll	212
Charlotte Polonaise	213
Dolly Varden	213
Delicate Cake 1 & 2	214
Coffee Cake 1 & 2	214
Fruit Cake	215-216
Hash Cake	216
Lady's Cake	216
Minnehaha Cake	217
Improved Sunshine Cake	217
Scotch Cake	217
Woolly Cake	217
Snow Ball Cake	218
Cream Puffs	218
White Fruit Cake, 1, 2 & 3	218
Blackberry Cake	219
Brides Loaf	219
Brod Torte	219
Buttermilk Cake	219
Short Cake, Strawberry	220
Orange Cake	220
Silver Cake, 1 & 2	220
Iowa Cake	221
Caramel Cake, 1 & 2	221
Vermont Pork Cake	221
Wedding Cake	222
Sponge Cake, 1 & 2	222
Velvet Cake	222
Angel Food Cake	223
Bread Cake	223
Bread Batter Cake	223
Currant Cake	223
Plain Cake	224

INDEX:—Continued

Cocoanut Pound Cake	224
Gold Cake	225
Nut Cake	225
Banana Cake	225
Brooklyn Cake	225
New Years Marble Cake	226
Fig Cake	226
Fig Layer Cake	226
Cup Cake	227
Cream Cake	227
Every Day Cake	227
Composition Cake	227
Ribbon Cake	228
Cream Layer Cake	228
Cookies, (various kinds)	228-229
Cocoanut Drops	229
Hermits, 1 & 2	229-230
Sunshines	230
Hounds Ears or Magic Pastry	230
Crinkles	230
Ginger Snaps, 1, 2 & 3	230-231
Ginger Drop Cookies	231
Corn Starch Patties	231
Velvet Cake	231
Jumbles, 1 & 2	231-232
Gingerbread, (various kinds)	232
Doughnuts	233
Crullers	233
Fritters, (various kinds)	233-234
Neapolitan Cake	235
White Fruit Cake	235
Blueberry Cake	235
Healthful Shortcake	235
Cocoanut Cake, 1 & 2	236
Marble Cake	236
Blackberry Jam Cake	237
Perfection Cake	237
Fruit Cake	237
Sponge Cake	237-238
Jelly Roll	230
Lady Fingers	238
Snow Flake Cake	238
Sunshine Cakes	230

CANDIES

Peanut Candy	255
Cocoanut Candy	255
Chocolate Creams	255
Cocoanut Cream Drops	255
English Walnut Candy	256
Caramels	256
Chocolate Caramels	256
Maple Caramels	256
Marsh Mallows	256
Molasses Taffy	257
Molasses Candy	257
Butter Scotch	257
Cream Candy	257
Salted Almonds	257

DESSERT DISHES

Gelatine Pudding	195
Snow Pudding, 1 & 2	195-196
Vanilla Snow	196
Spanish Cream	196
Russian Cream, 1 & 2	196-197
Chantilla Cream	197
Orange Jelly	197
Wine Jelly, 1 & 2	197
Lemon Jelly, 1 & 2	197-198
Lemon Foam, 1 & 2	198
Floating Island	198
Rule for Making Custard	199
Boiled Custard	199
Baked Custard	199
Pineapple Sponge	200
Tutti Frutti Sponge	200
Apricot Charlotte	200
Apple Charlotte	200
Tapioca Pudding, (various kinds)	201-202
Hens Nest	203
Paradise Hash	203
Dates Stuffed	203
Date Souffle	203
Dessert Trifle	204
Charlotte Russe, 1 & 2	204
Fried Apples	202
Raisin Puffs	205
Cream Puffs	205
Apple Lemon	205
Apple Jelly	205
Coffee Jelly	206
Ginger Apples	206
Apple Snowballs	206
Compote of Apples	206
Apples in Port Wine	207
Pink Apple Snow	207
Apple Float	207

ENTREES

Calves Brains	81
Sweet Breads	81
Mock Smelts	81
Little Pigs in Blankets	82
Breakfast Relish or Oysters	82
Salmon Loaf	82
Escalloped Ham	83
Escalloped Chicken	83
Potted Beef	83
Rice Pone	84

EGGS AND OMELETTES

Eggs, (various ways)	97 to 102
Omelettes	102
Oyster Omelettes, 1 & 2	102
Meat Omelette	103
Individual Omelette	103
Bread Omelette	103
Light Omelette	104
Rice Omelette	104
To Preserve Eggs	104
To Test Eggs	105
To Make an Egg Tester	105

FISH

To Fry Fish	21-22
Codfish, (various styles)	22-23

INDEX:—Continued.

Boiled Salmon.... 23
Broiled Salmon or other Salt Fish. 24
Salmon Gratin.... 24
Salmon Pudding.... 24
Broiled Fresh Mackerel.... 24
Boiled Salt Mackerel.... 25
Broiled Black Bass.... 25
Broiled Shad.... 25
Baked Shad.... 25
Escalloped Shad Roes.... 25
Baked Sturgeon.... 26
Baked White Fish.... 26
Stewed Sole.... 26
Fricasseed Eels.... 26
Fried Eels.... 27
Haddock Souffle.... 27
Baked Pickerel.... 27
Escalloped Lobsters.... 27
Fried Frogs.... 28
Escalloped Fish.... 28
Cold Boiled Fish.... 28
Baked Fish.... 28
Stuffing for Fish.... 29
Turbot a la Creme.... 29-30

FISH, Shell

Oysters.... 33, 34 and 35
Roast Clams.... 35
Stewed Clams.... 35
Crabs.... 35
Soft Shell Crabs.... 36
Deviled Crabs, Hard Shell.... 36
Lobsters.... 36-37

FROSTINGS AND FILLINGS FOR CAKES.

Rocky Mountain Filling.... 241
Orange Filling.... 241
Raisin Filling.... 241
Chocolate Filling.... 242
Fig Filling.... 242
Filling for Fig Cake.... 242
Fig Filling without Almonds.... 242
Lemon Jelly Filling.... 242
Almond Nougat Filling.... 242
Almond Filling.... 242
Caramel Filling.... 243
Cream Filling.... 243
Yellow Filling.... 243
Boiled Frosting.... 246
Maple Sugar Frosting.... 243
Milk Frosting.... 243
Chocolate Frosting.... 243
Caramel Frosting.... 244
Chocolate Icing.... 244
Macaroon Frosting.... 244

HOW—

To Remove Mildew from Linen.. 276
To Make Chewing Gum.... 276
To Make Caramel.... 276
To Make Coloring for Confect'ry.. 276
To Make Butter.... 277
To take Stains out of White Goods, 277
To Prepare Fruit for Canning.... 278

ICES, SHERBERTS AND ICE CREAMS.

Sherbet, (various kinds).... 247-248
Bisque.... 248
Ices, (various kinds).... 248-250
Roman Punch.... 250
Ice Creams.... 250 to 252
Orange Souffle.... 252
Tutti Frutti.... 252

MEATS

Beef (various ways).... 41 to 47
Veal "   "   .... 47 to 51
Mutton "   "   51
Pork, "   "   .... 52 to 54
Boston Baked Beans.... 54
Dumpling for Pot Pie.... 55
Meat Pie.... 55

MACARONI AND CHEESE

Baked Macaroni.... 159
Oysters and Macaroni.... 159
Macaroni with Cream Sauce.... 160
Macaroni with Tomato Sauce.... 160
Fondue.... 160
Cheese Fondue.... 160
Cheese Straws.... 161
Cheese Toast.... 161
Cheese Scollop.... 161
Cheese Ramakin.... 161
Schmier Kase.... 162
Welse Rarebit.... 162
Fried Cream.... 162

ODDS AND ENDS

Strawberry Jam.... 267
Baking Powder Biscuits.... 267
Grape Jam.... 267
Fruit Gelatine.... 268
Fruit Salad.... 268
Breakfast Buns.... 268
Brown Bread.... 269
Hermits.... 269
Snow Pudding.... 269
Cookies.... 269
Graham Pudding.... 269
Sole.... 270
Souffle for Soup.... 270
Brouchee Salpicon.... 270
Golden Cream.... 270
Vanilla Souffle.... 271
Custard Souffle.... 271
Wafer Pudding.... 271
Macaroni Pudding.... 272
Spanish Bun Cake.... 272
Orange Marmalade.... 272
Cocoa Bon Bons.... 272
Albany Rolls.... 273
Cocoanut Jelly Cake.... 273
Cream Nectar.... 273
Pickelette.... 273
Chocolate Frosted Cake.... 274
Graham Gems.... 274
Cabbage Pickles.... 274
Hollandaise Potatoes.... 274
Mikado Ice Cream.... 274
Raspberry Fritters.... 275
Strawberry Pancakes.... 275

INDEX:—Continued.

POULTRY AND GAME

Chicken, (various ways)	57 to 60
Stuffing for Chicken, Duck or Turkey	60
Prairie Chicken Roasted	60
Broiled Pheasant	60
Broiled Partridge	60
Broiled Squabs	60
Broiled Quail on Toast	61
Roast Quail	61
Stewed Pigeons	61
How to Cook Duck	61
Wild Duck	61
Roast Wild Duck	62
Roast Duck, Tame	62
Roast Goose	62
Boiled Turkey	63
Roast Turkey	63

PATTIES

Chicken Patties	93
Oyster Patties	94
Beef or Veal Patties	94
Sweetbread Patties	95

PASTRY AND PIES

Rules for Making Pies	165
Pie Crust	166
Pies, (various kinds)	166 to 175

PUDDINGS

Kiss Pudding	175
Indian Pudding	175
Spanish Pudding	176
Fig Pudding	176
Strawberry Pudding	177
Suet Pudding, 1, 2 & 3	177-178
Black Pudding	178
Steamed Apple Pudding	178
Apple Sago	178
Apple Pudding	179
Apple Batter Pudding	179
Apple Meringue Pudding	179
Corn Starch Pudding	179
Chocolate Pudding	180
Cherry Pudding	180
Iced Cherry Pudding with Cream	180
Caramel Pudding	181
Orange Pudding	181
Rice Pudding	181
Florentine Pudding	182
Oxford Pudding	182
Steamed Berry Pudding	182
Amber Pudding	182
Peach Meringue Pudding	183
Peach Cobbler	183
Peach Pudding	183
Dandy Pudding	183
Steamed Graham Pudding	184
Danish Pudding	184
Cottage Pudding	184-185
Bread Pudding	185
Cake Pudding	185
English Plum Pudding	185-186
Date Pudding	186
Queen Pudding	186
Mabels Apricot Pudding	186
Bread and Butter Pudding	187
Cocoanut Pudding	187
Roly Poly Pudding	187
Yorkshire Pudding	188
Apple Dumpling	188
Steamed Apple Dumpling	188
Peach Dumpling	189

PUDDING SAUCES

Foamy Sauce	191
Brandy Sauce	191
Banana Sauce	191
Hard Sauce	191
Vinegar Sauce	192
Home Made Sauce	192
Good Sauce	192
Strawberry Sauce	192
Wine Sauce	192
Vanilla Sauce	192
Cream Sauce	193
Plain Sauce	193
Pudding Sauce	193

SOUPS

Stock	7
Mutton and Lamb Broth	8
Pea Soup	8
Bean Soup	9
Barley Soup	9
Tomato Soup	9
Potato Soup	10
Puree of Potato Soup	10
Consomme	10
Vegetable Soup	11
Beef Soup with Vegetables	11
Codfish Soup	11
Macaroni Soup	11
Vermicelli Milk Soup	12
Oxtail Soup	12
Julienne Soup	12
Bouillon	13
Chicken Broth	13
Oyster Cream Soup	13
Cream of Asparagus Soup	14
Cream of Green Pea Soup	14
Tomato Cream Soup	14
Cream of Corn Soup	15
Chicken Cream Soup	15
Cream of Celery Soup	15-16
To Color Soups	16
Egg Balls for Soup	16
Noodles for Soup	17
Clam Chowder	17
Fish Chowder	17
Lobster Bisque	17

SAUCES

Bread Sauce	65
Brown Sauce	65
Fish Sauce	65
Anchovy Sauce	66
Waitre d'Hotel Sauce	66
Curry Sauce	66
Currant Jelly Sauce	66

INDEX:—Continued.

Hollandaise Sauce..	66
Mushroom Sauce....	67
Parsley Sauce......	67
Tomato Sauce......	67
Excellent Cream Sauce.....	67
Caper Sauce........	68
Mint Sauce........	68
Oyster Sauce......	68
Cream Sauce......	68
Egg Sauce........	68
Drawn Butter......	69
Chili Sauce........	69
India Sauce........	69
Mrs. Drake's Cranberry Sauce...	69
Apple Sauce........	70
Stewed Dried Fruit......	70
To Brown Flour......	70
To Brown Batter......	70
Vinagrette Sauce......	71
Celery Sauce........	71
Oyster Sauce for Turkey........	71
Sour Gravy........	71

SALADS AND DRESSINGS

Fish Salad........	73
Cucumber Salad......	73
Salmon Salad......	73
Salmon Salad for ½ can......	74
Chicken Salad......	74
Cabbage Salad..	75
Potato Salad..	75
Beef Salad. .	75
Tomato Salad......	75
Summer Salad..	76
Lobster Salad......	76
Shrimp Salad......	76
Lettuce Salad......	76
Fruit Salad	76
Dressings. (various kinds)......	77-79

SPICES, PICKLES AND CATSUP

Spiced Grapes........	129
Spiced Cherries......	129
Spiced Gooseberries	129
Spiced Peaches......	129
Spiced Currants......	130
Pickled Pears......	130
Pickled Crab Apples........	130
Pickled Peaches......	130
Ripe Cucumber Pickles......	130-131
Chopped Cucumber Pickles......	132
Piccalilli...	132
Chopped Green Tomatoes......	132
Green Tomato Pickles......	133
Sweet Tomato Pickles......	133
Tomato Butter......	133
Tomato Relish......	133
Tomato Catsup......	134
Gooseberry Catsup......	134
Grape Catsup......	134
Shirley Sauce	134

VEGETABLES

Stewed Mushrooms......	107
Broiled Mushrooms......	107-108
Potatoes (various ways)	109 to 112
Roasted Sweet Potatoes......	112
Boiled Sweet Potatoes......	112
Fried Sweet Potatoes......	113
Escalloped Sweet Potatoes......	113
Cauliflower......	113
Creamed Cauliflower......	113
Buttered Parsnips	114
Fried Parsnips......	114
Asparagus......	114
Celery........	114
Celery Salad......	115
Creamed Celery......	115
Turnips Mashed......	115
Yellow Turnips......	115
Summer Squash......	115
Winter Squash Boiled	115
Winter Squash Baked......	116
Green Corn......	116
Escalloped Corn......	116
Green Corn Pudding......	116
Corn Pudding......	116
Corn Oysters......	117
Baked Corn......	117
Green Corn Stewed......	117
Green Corn Cakes......	117-118
Succotash......	118
Ragout of Peas......	118
Green Peas......	118
To Cook Canned Peas......	119
Ripe Peas......	119
Puree of Peas......	119
Hygenic Baked Beans......	119
String Beans......	120
Butter Beans..	120
Lima Beans......	120
Boston Baked Beans......	121
Carrots Buttered......	121
Creamed Carrots......	121
Beets........	122
Beet Greens......	122
Beets Pickled......	122
Boiled Cabbage Creamed......	122
Fried Cabbage......	123
Boiled Cabbage......	123
Tomatoes Sliced......	123
Tomato Salad......	123
Baked Tomatoes......	123
Cream Tomatoes......	123
Fried Tomatoes......	124
Stewed Tomatoes......	124
Tomatoes on Toast......	124
Escalloped Tomatoes......	124
To Peel Tomatoes......	124
Egg Plant......	125
Cucumbers......	125
Dressed Spinach......	125
Spinach......	126
Boiled Dandelions......	126
Lettuce......	126
Lettuce Salad......	126
Vegetable Oysters......	127
Kale........	127
Boiled Onions......	127
Baked Onions......	127
Fried Onions......	127

Has it ever occurred to you that you can do your neighbors a good turn by telling them how to get Gillett's Magic Cook Book? They may not be using Magic Yeast, or may not be saving their red tickets. Remember every package of Magic Yeast is guaranteed to make perfect bread. When sending for Yeast tell them to get the Owl and Moon Brand called Magic.

SOUPS.

Stock.

Four pounds of shin of beef, four pounds knuckle of veal, any bones or trimmings of poultry or fresh meat, one-half pound of lean bacon or ham, two ounces of butter, two large onions stuck with cloves, three carrots, one head celery, one turnip, one bay leaf, two ounces salt, half a teaspoonful of whole pepper, a pinch of mace, a bunch of thyme and savory, and four quarts and a half pint of cold water.

Cut up the meat and bacon or ham into small pieces, cover with a pint of cold water and let simmer slowly, skim off the scum, then add the other ingredients and the four quarts and one-half pint of water, and let boil for five hours, remove the scum and set to cool; when cold, again remove the scum, and strain. This will form into jelly and can be kept a long time in a cool place, and is the basis of many of our soups.

White Stock.

Six pounds of knuckle of veal, half a pound of bacon (lean), small piece of butter, two onions, two turnips, two carrots, pinch of mace, four cloves stuck into the onion, small bunch of thyme and savory, pepper and salt, one tablespoonful of flour, and six quarts of water. Cut up the meat and the bacon and crack all the bones, slice the vegetables and herbs and add two quarts of water, and put on to boil. Let simmer slowly and take off the scum as it rises; then at the end of an hour add the rest of the water—one gallon. Let it cook steadily four hours, strain and set away to cool, in an earthen jar. This forms a basis for all the white soups used.

Mutton Broth.

Boil a piece of lean lamb or mutton for two or three hours in about four quarts of water, keeping the pot closely covered. Then soak one-half cup of rice and put in the soup; let boil for an hour, then put a well beaten egg in a cup of cold milk. thickened with a little flour, put in a little of the scalding liquor to prevent the egg from curdling the soup. Take out the meat and stir in this mixture, season with pepper, salt, thyme and a little parsley, let boil and serve.

Mutton Broth No. 2.

Boil one pound of lean loin of mutton with three pints of water for three hours; salt to taste: pour out the broth into a basin and when it is cold skim off the fat. It can be warmed up as wanted. This is the first preparation of animal diet that should be given during convalesence from any severe fever.

Mutton or Lamb Broth.

Take the water in which a leg of mutton or lamb was boiled in on the previous day, take off the fat and boil it two hours, with a turnip, an onion and a carrot cut fine, add some minced parsley and a spoonful of rice. All these except the parsley should be put in while the water is cold.

Pea Soup.

Put a pint of split peas to soak over night. About three hours before dinner pour off the water and add two quarts of water, a carrot, an onion, a little celery or celery seeds and a small piece of salt pork. Boil it steadily and be careful to stir it often lest it should burn; have boiling water at hand to add as the water boils away much faster in pea soup than in any other kind; strain it through a coarse sieve. A cup of milk added after the soup is done is an improvement.

Bean Soup.

Soak a quart of beans over night, cover with three quarts of water, and let boil with a piece of salt pork for several hours; season with celery, pepper and salt and strain through a colander. Croutons are very nice served with the soup.

Barley Soup.

Made the same as bean soup.

Tomato Soup.

One pint tomatoes, salt, two quarts water; boil one hour, then add one teaspoonful of soda, one pint milk, one-half pint rich cream, pepper and salt; let come to a boil; pour on rolled crackers.

Tomato Soup No. 2.

One can tomatoes, one bay leaf, one small onion, one pint water, one tablespoonful butter, two tablespoonfuls corn starch, one-quarter teaspoonful soda, one teaspoonful sugar, little parsley, salt and pepper to taste. Put the tomatoes, bay leaf, parsley, onion and water on to boil for a few minutes, then strain through a colander; rub the corn starch and butter together and when smooth, stir into the boiling soup. When smooth, add soda. salt, pepper and sugar; serve at once.

Potato Soup.

Four large potatoes, one small onion into which six cloves have been stuck, one piece celery; cook until potatoes fall to pieces, then take out the onions and celery and mash potatoes fine; pour enough boiling milk on the potatoes to make them the consistency of cream. Beat one egg and take a tablespoonful of butter, strain soup into this, season and stir well; serve immediately.

Potato Soup No. 2.

Four large potatoes, one onion; boil in two quarts of water until soft; press through a sieve and add one pint sweet milk, one tablespoon butter, salt and pepper to taste. Boil up again and serve.

Puree of Potato Soup.

Boil five or six potatoes with a little celery and onions, pass through a colander and add one-quarter pound of butter and enough hot milk to make it the consistency of thick cream; pepper and salt to taste. Chop fine a little parsley and throw in; boil one minute and serve.

Consomme.

Four pounds of beef, four pounds of veal, four quarts cold water, two ounces bacon, six cloves, a bunch of herbs, one tablespoonful salt, three onions, one carrot one turnip, two stalks celery, a little parsley, three eggs, a little celery salt, one lemon (juice and rind); wipe and cut the meat and bones into small pieces, then strain carefully and set away to cool, then strain off all the fat and it is ready for use. This can be clarified and colored same as bouillon.

Vegetable Soup.

Three quarts of stock, two carrots, two turnips, two potatoes, one quart and a pint of boiling water, two tomatoes, one-half cup of rice or barley, a stalk of celery, a little chopped cabbage. Put on the stock and boiling water to heat, chop the vegetables and add them and the rice, and let boil for a few minutes until tender, add pepper and salt to taste. This may be strained or not, just as you wish. If strained, it is nice served with croutons.

To make croutons, toast slices of stale bread, then put a small piece of butter in a sauce pan, cut up the toast in small pieces, put in the pan and brown.

Beef Soup with Vegetables.

Take beef or veal bone, put in one gallon cold water; boil five hours, add salt and pepper; skim as is necessary, strain, set in a cool place over night. Skim next day; chop piece of cabbage, two medium sized potatoes, one small carrot, one turnip and one onion together; add one tablespoonful rice, one can tomatoes strained; put all in a vessel, boil until soft, serve hot.

Codfish Soup.

One-quarter pound codfish cut in small squares, freshened by boiling in water once, after which boil again fifteen minutes; strain into a quart of milk, thicken with a teaspoonful of cornstarch. When it comes to a boil set aside, add yolk of one egg, season to taste, lastly add codfish, one-half tablespoonful Worcestershire sauce.

Macaroni Soup.

Break the macaroni into small pieces and put it on to cook in a stew pan, covering it with three pints of boiling water. Let it boil for about twenty minutes, drain and add it to three pints of stock which has been melted, add pepper and salt to taste.

Vermicelli Soup.

Put a quarter of a pound of vermicelli to soak in one quart of warm water, then add to it two quarts of white stock and a piece of butter. Let it boil about twenty minutes and serve.

Vermicelli Milk Soup.

Into a quart of boiling milk put a level salt spoonful of celery salt; stirring slowly, add two ounces of vermicelli and continue to stir twenty minutes. The yolks of two eggs thoroughly beaten should be added when the soup is ready to be removed from the fire. This soup may be flavored with cinnamon and sugar if desired. This is one of the most nutritious and non-stimulating articles of diet. Persons who partake of this soup are said to have no craving for strong drink.

Oxtail Soup.

Three oxtails, three small onions, one bay leaf, two carrots, two tablespoonfuls of flour, a turnip, a little pepper, add a gallon of water and set on to boil. Let it boil steadily for two hours, cut the meat off the bones and set aside; throw the bones back into the pot and boil for an hour longer, then strain carefully; rinse a half cup of rice and throw in; boil twenty minutes, then add the meat and serve.

Julienne Soup.

To make this favorite French soup, a small quantity of every description of vegetables should be used, including lettuce, sorrel and tarragon; however some few kinds of vegetables mixed together make a most estimable soup. Weigh half a pound of the vegetables, in fair proportions to each, that is, carrots, turnips, onions, celery and leeks, which cut into small fillets an inch in length and of the thickness of a trussing needle. When done, wash dry and pass them in butter and sugar; add two quarts of clear soup, adding just before it is done a little sorrel, cabbage, lettuce and chervil or peas, if handy.

Bouillon.

Cut up and break six pounds of beef and bone, put in it two quarts of water, allowing it to simmer slowly for about five hours. Strain through a very fine sieve, removing all fatty matter. Season with pepper and salt.

Chicken Broth.

The water chickens were boiled in, set away in a cool place, makes a good broth. The next day skim off all the fat; take the bones of the chicken, put into the soup pot with the broth, one onion cut very fine, one carrot, one turnip, a small bunch of parsley, a little salt and pepper; let it boil two hours, take out bones and add one-half cup of rice or vermicelli; let it boil one hour.

Oyster Cream Soup.

Look carefully over a quart of solid oysters, to free them from shells; put them on to cook in their own liquor, adding enough water to make a quart of liquor. Let them come to a boil, then rub the oysters through a sieve with a potato masher, moistening them with the liquor, and keep warm. Put two tablespoonfuls each of butter and flour in a sauce pan, stir until they bubble, add quart of boiling milk, stirring until quite smooth, then add the oyster pulps and liquor. When smooth, if thicker than cream, add more boiling milk, season with salt and pepper and boil once; serve with small crackers or croutons.

Cream of Asparagus Soup.

Wash one bunch of asparagus, tie up and put in a sauce pan of boiling water. Let it boil for three-quarters of an hour, take out the asparagus, cut off the tops and set aside until wanted. Put one quart of milk on to boil in a double boiler, then press the asparagus stalks through a colander and add them to the milk. Rub two tablespoonfuls of corn starch and one tablespoonful of butter together until smooth, add to the boiling milk and stir constantly until it thickens, then add the asparagus tops; salt and pepper to taste and serve. When you cannot get the fresh asparagus, canned asparagus may be used. Also one pint of white stock and one pint of milk instead of one quart of milk.

Cream of Green Pea Soup.

Boil a pint of shelled peas in a pint of water; when soft, take out one-half which mash through a colander, return the pulp to the water in which it was boiled and add three pints of milk, butter size of an egg, teaspoonful of sugar, pepper, salt and a pinch of mace. Let all boil and drop into it as many eggs as there are persons to be served, one at a time carefully, as for poaching; let simmer gently until eggs are cooked, then serve.

Tomato Cream Soup.

One pint of cooked tomatoes, one pint of boiling water, one pint of sweet milk and cream, one-half teaspoonful soda in the tomatoes; when done foaming add the water, then scald and strain; heat the milk, season with pepper, salt and butter, and put in the tomatoes, add rolled crackers if you like, or two teaspoonfuls of cornstarch.

Cream of Corn Soup.

One can corn, one quart and one-half pint of milk, three tablespoonfuls of butter, two tablespoonfuls of flour, one teaspoonful salt, one-quarter teaspoonful pepper, yolks of two eggs. Put the corn in a wooden bowl and mash it fine as possible, then put in a double boiler with one quart of milk and cook for twenty minutes; put the butter in a frying pan and cook slowly for ten minutes, then add the flour, cook until it becomes frothy, but do not burn; then add to the milk and corn; add next salt and pepper and cook ten minutes. Rub the soup through a strainer, beat the yolks of the eggs well and add to them one-half pint of cold milk; stir this mixture into the soup, cook for a minute or two, stirring constantly.

Chicken Cream Soup.

Cut up a medium-sized old chicken into quarters, with a piece of ham and an onion and add about four quarts of water. Let this slowly boil until the meat will drop off the bones, then add a half cup of rice well washed; add next some chopped parsley, salt and pepper. When the rice is tender, take out the meat and add two cups of rich milk thickened with a little flour.

Cream of Celery Soup.

Take two quarts of white stock, a small piece of butter, a small piece of lean ham and put on the stove to boil; chop the white part of the celery into small pieces and add it to the stock; let it boil for an hour, then drain through a sieve, add a pint of rich cream and thicken with a little flour. This is nice served with croutons.

Cream of Celery Soup No. 2.

One-half cup of rice, one cup of celery chopped fine and cooked in different stew pans until soft, when nearly ready to serve put together and add two quarts of milk, salt and pepper and small piece of butter. After heating thoroughly, pour into tureen, into which have been placed small squares of toasted bread.

Celery Cream Soup.

Boil a cupful of rice in three pints of milk until it will pass through a sieve. Grate the white parts of two heads of celery (three if small) on a bread grater, add this to the rice milk after straining; put to it a pint of strong white stock, allow to boil until celery is tender. Season with salt and cayenne pepper and serve. If cream is obtainable substitute one pint for same quantity of milk.

To Color Soups.

A fine amber color can be obtained by adding finely grated carrot to the clear stock when it is quite free from scum.

Red is obtained by using red skinned tomatoes from which the skin and the seeds have been strained out.

Spinach leaves pounded in a mortar, and the juice pressed out and added to the soup gives a green color.

Black beans make an excellent brown soup. The same color can be obtained by adding burnt sugar and browned flour to clear stock.

Egg Balls for Soup.

Boil four eggs, put into cold water, mash yolks with yolk of one raw egg and one teaspoonful of flour, pepper, salt and parsley; make into balls and boil two minutes.

Noodles for Soup.

Rub into two eggs as much flour as they will absorb, then roll out until as thin as a wafer; dust over a little flour, then roll over and over into a roll; cut off thin slices from the edge of the roll and shake out into long strips; put them into the soup lightly and boil for ten minutes; salt should be added while mixing with the flour—about a good-sized pinch.

Clam Chowder.

The materials needed are clams, salt pork, onions, potatoes, soda biscuit, plenty of seasoning and milk. First fry in chowder kettle, the salt pork, until nicely browned, in fat; after removing pork, fry onions; have clams ready and when onions are cooked, add water, and in alternate layers the soda biscuit, clam liquor and clams, potatoes, fried pork, chopped fine, and seasoning pepper, salt (and sweet herbs if liked). boil all together until potatoes are nearly done, when remove from kettle to a tureen; add a quart of milk and a little thickening to gravy; when scalded pour it over the contents of tureen and serve.

Fish Chowder.

Fry three or four pieces of salt pork in a deep kettle; when crisp, take out and put into kettle a layer of sliced potatoes, then one of fish, until all is used; pepper, add two onions cut fine, pour in boiling water enough to cover all; boil half hour, add half a pint of milk and cook five minutes longer. The best fish for chowder is haddock.

Lobster Bisque.

One can of lobsters, two cups of milk, three pints of boiling water, one tablespoonful of butter, one-half cup fine cracker crumbs, salt and pepper; chop the lobster rather coarse, taking care not to tear it; put boiling water, salt, pepper and lobster in a saucepan and cook gently for forty minutes. Have ready scalding milk in which the crumbs have soaked twenty minutes; stir in butter, then milk and crumbs, set in hot water five minutes and serve.

FISH.

Any fish out of season is unwholesome; you can always tell if the fish is eatable, by examining the eyes and scales; if the eyes are clear and the scales bright, and no unpleasant odor to it, it is in good condition, and should be cooked very soon after leaving the water, as the flesh becomes soft and turns color quickly.

Clean the fish as soon as possible and cover the inside with a sprinkling of salt and put in the ice box or a cool place until used. Salt fish should always be soaked over night to freshen them, but fresh fish should not be soaked unless frozen, when they need cold water poured over them to thaw them out.

The usual modes of cooking fish, are boiling, frying, baking or broiling; large fish are generally boiled and are sewn up into a bag, smaller fish are usually fried, and brook trout and smelts are served with the heads on; many consider that part quite a choice tid bit. In baking fish you need a slow fire, and to baste the fish often with butter and water, and some stuff it with a dry dressing of bread, butter, pepper and salt. Salmon is a very nutritious fish, and the most used of any and is usually boiled.

To Fry Fish.

Have ready your kettle of hot drippings or lard; clean the fish, cut out the back bone, season with salt and pepper, dip in flour or egg and cracker crumbs, and drop into the hot lard. When browned on one side, turn, and drain when done. This is delicious served with tomato sauce.

Boiled Salt Cod.

Put the fish to soak over night; in the morning change the water and wash off the salt. Put it on in cold water, then let it boil a half hour; drain and serve in a heated dish, with an egg sauce poured over it, or after draining off the water, pour a pint of milk over the fish; season with pepper, butter and a pinch of salt, if too fresh, and thicken with a little flour; lastly, drop in two eggs, stir quickly, and pour in heated dish.

Codfish Balls.

Take one pint of codfish picked fine, two pints potatoes, raw, and sliced thickly; boil until the potatoes are thoroughly done, then remove from the stove and drain; mash fine, add one tablespoon butter, one egg well beaten, a half cup rich cream or milk; put flour on your hands and roll into balls; have ready a kettle of hot lard and drop them in; when they are a nice brown they are done; garnish the platter with parsley and serve.

Boiled Fresh Cod.

Sew the fish in a thin cloth (cheese or mosquito netting); boil in salted water, allowing about eighteen minutes to the pound. Carefully unwrap serve with an egg sauce or oyster sauce.

Fried Fresh Cod.

Wash the steaks carefully, season, dip in egg and roll in bread or cracker crumbs, and fry in a hot batter.

Cod Omelet.

Break into small pieces the thickest parts of a dressed cod; season it with a little grated nutmeg and a little pounded mace; beat up six eggs well and mix with it, forming it into paste. Fry it as an omelet and serve as hot as possible.

Pate of Salt Cod.

Boil one cup oyster liquor, stir in two tablespoonfuls of cornstarch wet with cold milk, when it thickens add three tablespoonfuls of butter and a little pepper, then one of fish (which has been soaked, boiled and flaked) heat and stir in three chopped hard boiled eggs. Take from the fire and cover over a pot of boiling water fifteen minutes; line a buttered mold with puff paste, pricking at the bottom; cut a round piece for a cover and bake separately. Bake both in a quick oven; when almost cold turn out the shell and fill with fish, fit on the top and invert on a hot plate.

Codfish Croquettes.

Take one pint bowl of fish in strips and twice full of small potatoes pared, then drain off the water and mash very fine; when cool beat two eggs and add butter the size of an egg and a little pepper, beat all thoroughly, then have a kettle of hot lard and drop in with a spoon in an oblong shape; cook until a light brown.

Boiled Salmon.

Wash the fish well in cold water, wipe and sprinkle with salt, sew up nicely in a mosquito-net bag and put in a kettle and boil a quarter of an hour to the pound in hot salted water. When done, unwrap with care and lay upon a hot dish; garnish with slices of lemon or parsley or sliced eggs. Have ready a cupful of drawn butter, into which have been stirred two teaspoonfuls of chopped parsley and the juice of two lemons. Pour on the salmon and serve part in a boat.

Broiled Salt Salmon or other Salt Fish.

Soak in tepid or cold water twenty-four hours, changing water several times. If in a hurry, or desiring a very salt relish, it may do to soak a short time, having water warm and changing, parboiling slightly. At the hour wanted, broil sharply; season to suit taste, covering with butter. This recipe answers for all kinds of salt fish.

Salmon Gratin.

One cup of cold boiled salmon, flaked; mix with one-half cup of drawn butter; pepper and salt. Fill little earthen dishes with the mixture covered with fine bread crumbs, and brown.

Salmon Pudding.

Mince one can of salmon (saving liquor for sauce), put in four tablespoonfuls of melted butter, one-half cup of fine crumbs, pepper and salt and finally three well beaten eggs; put in buttered mold and set in a pan of hot water; cover and steam in oven for one hour, filling with boiling water as it evaporates. Set in cold water a minute and turn out.

Sauce.—Heat one cup of milk to boiling, and thicken with a tablespoonful of cornstarch wet in cold water; add one spoonful of butter, salmon liquor and one beaten egg; take from the fire, season, and stand in hot water three minutes, covered; add juice of half a lemon; pour over the pudding.

Broiled Fresh Mackerel.

Split the mackerel down the back, leaving the head on, wash carefully and wipe dry, sprinkle with pepper and salt; broil over a hot fire and lay on a heated dish; pour over the whole, melted butter.

Boiled Salt Mackerel.

Wash the fish thoroughly, put to soak with the meat side down; in the morning rinse in a couple of waters, boil a few minutes only in a kettle of hot water, take out carefully, sprinkle with pepper and salt and pour melted butter over it; some serve cream sauce with it.

Broiled Black Bass.

Wash the fish carefully, split down the back, dry with a cloth, and season well with salt and pepper; place on a broiler with the flesh down, cover with a dripping pan, and when nicely broiled, have ready some melted butter to pour over it. Halibut or salmon can be broiled the same way.

Broiled Shad.

Split, wash carefully and dry with a cloth; put on the greased gridiron with the flesh next the coals; cover with a pan, and broil carefully, then turn; pour plenty of melted butter over and serve; garnish with slices of lemon.

Baked Shad.

Wash the shad carefully and stuff with bread crumbs, pepper, salt, butter, little chopped parsley, add the beaten yolk of one egg to hold the stuffing together; tie a string around it and baste frequently with butter and water; serve with *Sauce Hollandaise*.

Roe.—Parboil in a small pan, drain, season well with salt, pepper, dredge with flour and fry like any fish.

Escalloped Shad Roes.

Boil the roes in water with a little vinegar; lay in cold water five minutes and then wipe dry; crumble but do not crush; set by; pound yolks of three hard boiled eggs to powder and beat into a cup of drawn butter; add seasoning and then the roes; pour into a layer of crumbs in a baking dish and cover with crumbs (about a cup of crumbs in all); stick dots of butter over the top, and bake covered until it begins to bubble; then brown on upper grating of the oven.

Baked Sturgeon.

Take a piece of sturgeon, about four pounds, wash well and parboil for fifteen minutes; then put in a pan with a little water and bake about an hour, putting plenty of butter over it occasionally. Serve with drawn butter.

Baked Whitefish.

Wash carefully, dry with a cloth and stuff with bread crumbs well seasoned; sew up with twine and put in a pan, with enough water to keep from scorching; baste frequently with butter and water, and serve with egg sauce.

Stewed Sole with Tomato Sauce.

Put a can of tomatoes in a sauce-pan with a teaspoonful of finely chopped onion, a dessertspoonful of salad oil and a little cayenne pepper and salt, simmer for half an hour, then lay in the fish, a flounder (usually called sole), adding a little water, if there be not sufficient liquor to cook; Beat up the yolk of an egg with the juice of a lemon, and five minutes before dishing the fish, pour it in and shake the sauce-pan to prevent curdling.

Fricasseed Eels.

Skin, clean and cut in two inch lengths; boil in water without quite covering until tender; add a piece of butter with a teaspoonful of wheat flour or crushed crackers worked into it, and a little chopped and scalded parsley with salt and pepper to taste, and a little vinegar if desired.

Fried Eels.

After skinning and cleaning the eels, cut in small pieces, wipe dry, roll in flour or dip in egg and roll in cracker crumbs, and fry the same as other fish, in hot salted lard, or drippings. Eels may be prepared the same and broiled.

Haddock Souffle.

One cup of cold baked haddock and one of mashed potatoes mixed together, one-half cup of milk added gradually, salt and pepper; stir in one egg, well beaten; put in a buttered mold or dish and set in the oven until very hot; then beat the white of another egg very stiff and stir into it the yolk beaten with salt and pepper; heap over the fish and brown.

Baked Pickerel.

Clean the fish and wipe it dry, and lay in the pan with sufficient hot water to keep from burning; have your stuffing ready, and fill in the centre and tie it up; baste frequently, as the oftener fish is basted the better it is when finished. Serve with an egg sauce and garnish with parsley and slices of lemon.

Escalloped Lobster.

For two and one-half pounds green lobster, use one pint cream, two tablespoonfuls flour, two of butter, a little cayenne pepper, salt to taste; a small pint of bread crumbs. Take the lobster from the shell, cut in small pieces; put the cream over to boil, saving enough to blend the flour. When boiled, add the flour and butter. Let boil ten minutes, then add the lobster and boil one minute; add salt and pepper. Now butter your individual dish and fill, sprinkle over each with bread crumbs and bake until slightly brown. Serve hot.

Fried Frogs.

There is only one part of the frog that is used as food, and that is the hind legs; when gathered they must be skinned and put into boiling water for a few minutes, then thrown in cold water or put on ice until cold; season with pepper and salt, roll in flour or dip in egg and cracker crumbs, and fry brown in butter.

Escalloped Fish.

Any cold fish left from dinner may be used. Pick up the fish, being very careful about removing all the bones.

Put one pint of milk in a double boiler, add a few slices of onion, a little parsley chopped fine, small piece of butter, little pepper and salt; when hot, stir in two tablespoonfuls either of corn starch or flour, which has been dissolved in a little cold milk; let it come to a boil, then remove; rub the inside of the dish with butter; first put a layer of fish, then the cream, then sprinkle cracker crumbs, so on until the dish is full, putting a layer of crumbs on top to keep the milk from scorching. This is a nice way to use up cold fish.

Cold Boiled Fish a la Vinagrette.

Take the skin and bones out and place in the center of a dish; have two hard-boiled eggs cut fine, sprinkle the fish with this and garnish with small lettuce leaves, water cresses, cold boiled potatoes or beets cut in slices, with here and there a sprig of parsley. Serve the vinagrette sauce in a separate dish, garnish and pour a spoonful of the sauce over each dish as you serve it. A nice dish for tea or lunch in summer and takes the place of a salad.

Baked Fish.

Fish will cook better if placed upright in the pan, instead of on one side. Fish that are flat like shad may be kept in place by propping up with stale bread or pared potatoes. Others may be made into shape of letter "S." Run a threaded needle through the head, middle of body and tail, and draw string, fasten the ends. Thus prepared fish will keep their shape and can be better served. In putting fish to bake, rub the pan well with salt pork, and put small pieces of pork under the fish, which will prevent it from sticking. Baste often with pork fat; bake until brown.

Stuffing for Fish Weighing from Four to Six Pounds.

One cup cracker crumbs, one saltspoonful salt, one saltspoonful pepper, one teaspoonful chopped onions, one teaspoonful chopped parsley, one teaspoonful capers, one teaspoonful pickles, one-quarter cup melted butter. This makes a dry, crumbly stuffing. If a moist stuffing is desired use stale bread (not dried) crumbs and moisten with one beaten egg and the butter, or moisten the crackers with warm water. If an oyster stuffing is desired, use one pint oysters, one cup of seasoned and buttered cracker crumbs; drain and roll each oyster in the crumbs; fill the fish with the oysters and sprinkle the remainder of the crumbs over the oysters.

Turbot A La Crème.

Boil fish with plenty of salt in water; take off the skin, being careful to keep it whole; boil one onion and a bunch of parsley in pint of milk; take four tablespoonfuls flour, one tablespoonful butter, mix well; add one pint of cream or milk; strain out the onion and parsley and add to the flour mixture; let it all boil five minutes, then add a pinch of mace and one tablespoonful anchovy sauce; grease a deep dish with butter, put spoonful of sauce on the bottom, then a layer of fish, so alternately until the dish is full; sprinkle bread crumbs on top with small pieces of butter; bake in a moderate oven a half hour.

Turbot A La Crème No. 2.

Dressing.—Boil one quarter pound of butter with one quart milk, penny's worth of parsley chopped fine, flour to make the consistency of cream, salt and pepper to taste. Four pounds fish; boil fish until done, remove skin and bones, pick to pieces; put in baking dish a layer of fish, then a layer of the dressing, etc., until the dish is filled, then a layer of crackers on top; bake one-half hour.

SHELL FISH.

Oysters.

Oysters are in season from September to May. The Blue Points are considered the choicest for serving raw. These are served on the half-shell and usually six to a person.

Blue Points on the Half-Shell.

Wash half a dozen shells carefully, then slip a knife between the upper and under shell and open, allowing them to remain on the under shell. Serve on a plate and eat with lemon and horseradish.

Plain Stew.

Make the same as a milk stew, leaving out the milk and adding more butter.

Pan Oysters.

Select some large oysters and lay in the bottom of a dripping pan, then pour over them a little of their own liquor, enough to keep them from burning. Place in a hot oven and let them get hot; place on buttered toast, moisten with the hot juice; add pepper, salt and butter and serve.

Stewed Oysters.

Drain a quart of oysters and put the liquor on the stove with a half teacupful boiling water, a little salt and pepper and let boil up once. Then add the oysters, a piece of butter size of an egg, a half pint of boiling milk and let it come to a boil. Serve while hot and if too thin add a little flour for thickening. Serve cold slaw and crackers with this dish.

Creamed Oysters.

Boil one-half can of nice oysters in their own liquor for one minute, then drain and put on a cup of cream and a cup of milk in rice boiler, when hot add a tablespoonful of corn starch and a piece of butter rubbed together until smooth, to the hot cream; when it is thick add the oysters, pepper and salt, stir until all are heated, then serve.

Escalloped Oysters.

Line a baking dish with butter, then have ready a dish of bread crumbs, put first a layer of crumbs, then a layer of oysters, butter in little pieces, salt and pepper; repeat until the dish is full, being careful to have the crumbs on top, with small pieces of butter. Moisten with milk and a little of the oyster liquor. Bake until a good brown, in a hot oven and serve in the same dish.

Broiled Oysters.

Pick out large fat oysters, dry carefully and season well with salt and pepper, place on the broiler turn on the other side when browned and drop into a hot dish and pour melted butter over them. Some serve them on squares of buttered toast.

Fried Oysters.

Pick out very large fat oysters for frying, clean, drain and dry on a soft cloth, season well with salt and pepper; dip in beaten egg and roll in bread crumbs and drop in hot lard. Drain carefully on a piece of brown paper, then serve in a hot dish immediately.

Scallops.

There is only one part of this fish fit to use, that is the muscular part. They are sold by measure same as clams and prepared about the same.

Fried Scallops.

Wash in boiling water, then drain; dry carefully, season with salt and pepper, dip in egg and roll in cracker crumbs and fry in hot lard.

Roast Clams.

If at a clam-bake, the clams are left in the shells and roasted on hot stones; then open, empty juice into a pan, add the clams, pepper, butter and a pinch of salt. If at home roast in a pan over a hot fire, or put in the oven to roast and fix same as above.

Stewed Clams.

Put one-half peck of clams in a kettle with a little hot water and the steam will open the shell. Then take out of the shell and strain the liquor and put in with the clams again. When it has come to a boil add one cup of milk, a piece of butter the size of an egg, two crackers well rolled and salt and pepper to taste.

Crabs.

Crabs are sold alive, like the lobster, or boiled.

Soft Shell Crabs.

Soft-shell crabs are the hard-shell crabs after they have shed their shell, as it becomes hard again in a few days; the supply is usually very scarce.

Fried Soft Shell Crabs.

Clean well and scrape out the fins under the shell; fry in lard and butter mixed until they become a little crisp. Serve on toast with melted butter poured over and a little parsley to garnish the dish with.

Deviled Crabs, Hard-Shell.

Take six fresh crabs, boil and chop fine, two tablespoonfuls of butter, a little mustard powder, salt and pepper to taste. Put the meat into a dish and rub into it an equal quantity of bread crumbs. Mix the butter to a cream, then stir the mustard into it, add the crab meat, crumbs and a tablespoonful of cream, a little cayenne and salt to taste. Fill the crab shell with the mixture; put little pieces of butter on top and sprinkle with bread crumbs and brown in the oven.

Lobsters.

To pick out a lobster: you will find the heaviest are the best; never purchase boiled lobster, but the freshest and most lively ones you can get. To test the freshness of the lobster: the claws will have a strong motion when the eyes are pressed with the fingers and they will be very lively. The lobster is not thoroughly cooked unless it turns a bright red color. They are very indigestible however and should be avoided by dyspeptics.

Steamed Lobster.

To steam a lobster put it in a steamer, over a fish kettle, and steam until it turns a very bright red. Serve with lettuce and salad.

Deviled Lobster.

Deviled lobster is made the same as deviled crabs, using one cup of lobster chopped fine instead of half a dozen crabs. This takes one small lobster. Serve with shells.

MEATS.

A person should be very careful about cooking meats of all kinds, and it is most essential that they select the best.

BEEF should be smooth, of a clear red color, and tender, when pinched with the finger; and the fat should be white.

Sirloins, ribs, and pin bone are the best parts for roasting.

VEAL should have a pinkish tinge; and the calf should not be killed till it is two months old, then the flesh is firm; before that time the flesh has a bluish look, and is flabby, and soft.

MUTTON is best, when the flesh is a bright red, very juicy, the grain firm, and close, and the fat firm and white.

PORK is decidedly unwholesome, and very indigestible for dyspeptics, and is chiefly used in cold weather, and it needs to be well cooked as a piece of rare pork is very injurious.

LAMB is similar in looks to mutton, of a bright red color, and with white fat. Lamb is only in season from April until September, and should be about the age of veal, two months old. Lamb should be very thoroughly cooked, and is best roasted, though some fry the chops, even if they are very small.

Roast Beef.

Some prefer the first three ribs of beef for roasting, but for myself, I prefer the third, forth and fifth, but for a small family the first are more suitable. Do not take out the bone; but have your butcher chop it twice, and rub well with pepper, and salt, and dredge lightly with flour. If you do not use an improved roaster, place in a dripping pan, and pour a cupful of water into it.

It does not take over an hour to cook an ordinary sized roast, and most persons prefer it medium rare; when done, place on a heated dish; then heat the gravy, and thicken with some browned flour and a little boiling water. Serve in a gravy boat.

Roast Beef with Yorkshire Pudding.

Bake exactly as directed for an ordinary roast beef, for the table, then make a Yorkshire pudding to eat with the roast, as follows: For every pint of milk, take three eggs, three cups of flour, a little salt, stir to a smooth batter, and pour into the dripping pan, under the meat, a half hour before it is done.

Pot Roast.

Get a piece of beef about six pounds in weight, but not too fat. Wash and put in the pot with a little water, let it cook slowly, and add a little pepper and salt, keep it cooking slowly until tender, let the water boil down and take the meat out of the pot, and what gravy there may be. Put a piece of butter in the pot, sprinkle a little flour on the meat, return to the pot and let it brown. Pour the gravy back into the kettle, add a little water, and flour to thicken it, then serve.

To Corn Beef.

Rub the beef with salt and a little saltpetre, until the salt lies dry upon it; put in a cool place for twenty-four hours, then repeat, and put away until the next day.

For the pickle, take three gallons of water, two ounces of saltpetre, one-half gallon of salt, and three-quarters of a pound of brown sugar. Boil this brine a few minutes, then set away to cool. When the brine is cold, wipe the beef dry, and pour the pickle over it. This ought to keep the beef for some time.

Corn Beef Hash.

Three cups of boiled corned beef, chopped fine, one and one-half cups of mashed or chopped potatoes, milk, salt, pepper and melted butter. Put this in a frying pan, stir until it is smoking hot, then put it in a dish, and serve with poached eggs put on top of the hash.

Beef Stew.

Cut the beef in small pieces, put into a sauce-pan, with water enough to cover it, stew for an hour or so, then set away until the next morning; then season with salt, pepper, a little chopped onion, and if liked, a little parsley. Then let it stew for about one hour, add a little browned flour, dissolved in water, a little Worcestershire sauce, boil up once and serve.

Beef Tongue Boiled.

Select a nice large tongue, put in a kettle with water, a little salt, cook five or six hours, put into cold water and skin.

Smoked Beef Tongue Boiled.

Wash well, and put to soak in cold water over night. In the morning put on the stove in a kettle of cold water, and simmer for several hours, until tender. Let it cool in the liquor it has been boiled in; then remove the skin, and it is ready to serve.

Beef Loaf.

Three pounds beef, half pound salt pork, three or four eggs well beaten, small bowl rolled crackers, or bread crumbs, salt and pepper to taste, a little sage, small piece of butter. Mix well together, add cold water until you think it is about right, there is no rule for that. Bake one hour to one and one-half hours.

Beef Turn-Over.

Mince fine and season cold beef, three eggs, one cup of milk, flour to make good batter (about four table spoonfuls), heat two tablespoonfuls butter in skillet, mix parsley, pepper and salt in batter to pour in skillet. As soon as it forms, pour in meat; turn corners to make the turn-over; turn over in skillet, and when thoroughly cooked slice upon a hot platter.

Dried Beef on Toast.

Chip the beef very thin, place in a sauce-pan, add a little butter, and milk, thicken with flour dissolved in water, add a little pepper, and pour over buttered squares of toast.

Breakfast Chipped Beef.

Put some milk and water on the stove, with a beaten egg, and add a little flour, let this boil up well, then add the chipped beef. Do not cook more than a minute, if the beef is not too salt, it will be seasoned right.

Baked Beef's Heart.

This is prepared the same as the boiled heart. Fill with stuffing and put in the oven. Baste often with melted butter, and when done put in a hot dish. Make the gravy the same as for the boiled beef heart, and serve hot.

Stewed Kidneys.

Be careful to select nice fresh kidneys, cut them into slices, sprinkle pepper and salt, and fry a nice brown, then pour a little warm water in the pan, thicken with flour dissolved in water, a little chopped parsley, and add the kidneys. Let them stew gently and serve.

Beef's Heart with Stuffing.

Soak in cold water, then remove the inside strings or muscles, and fill with a stuffing made of two cups bread crumbs, two table spoonfuls melted butter, a little chopped parsley, sage, salt and pepper, mix well and fill the heart, tie tightly with twine and sew in a cloth, then fill the kettle with boiling water, and cook until tender. Take out of the cloth, and serve. Add a little butter and flour to the gravy, let boil, a pinch of salt and pepper added, and pour over the heart.

Fried Beef's Liver.

Pour boiling hot water over the pieces of liver, let them stand for five minutes then wipe carefully, sprinkle salt, pepper, and dip in flour, and fry. Lay thin slices of bacon in the pan, and when the fat is all out, fry the liver in it, cooking quickly. Thicken the gravy with a little browned flour, and pour over the liver.

Calves Liver Fried.

Prepare in the same way as beef liver, fry in bacon fat and serve with pieces of bacon nicely cooked.

Plain Hash.

Pieces of cold roasts, steaks, chops, or stews may be used, chopping them very fine. To every cup of meat add one onion, a piece of butter, salt and pepper to taste, and a little water. Chop the onion fine, add to the meat, put into the sauce-pan, add the butter, salt, pepper and water, stew for a few minutes, until the onion is cooked, and serve.

Plain Hash on Toast.

Toast pieces of bread and butter them, chop the meat fine; add a little butter, pepper, salt, water enough to cover, a little summer savory and flour, stir frequently, and pour over the toast

Broiled Hamburg Steak.

Chop the steak in small pieces, or let your butcher do it for you, place on your broiler, season with pepper and salt, and when finished, place on a hot platter, and pour melted butter over it.

Beefsteak Broiled.

Have ready a bed of hot coals, then grease the broiler with butter, place the steak on it, let it broil nicely on one side, then turn on the other. Season with pepper and salt, and place on a hot platter, and pour plenty of melted butter over it. There is no definite time for broiling a steak, as it depends on the thickness entirely. If it is to be served rare, of course the length of time will be much shorter.

Pin-bone, porterhouse, and sirloin are the best pieces for broiling.

Fried Beefsteak.

Have your frying pan very hot, then grease with butter, put your steak on, turn frequently, until done, put on a platter and season with pepper, salt, and butter, serve hot.

Beefsteak and Onions.

Prepare the steak like the preceding recipe. Peel a dozen onions cut in thin slices, then fry in a saucepan until brown. Put your steak on a platter, dish your onions around it, and on top, and let stand covered for a few moments, then send to the table hot.

Entree De Boeuf (Stew.)

Have a thick piece of beef; chop fine a medium sized onion and put in a kettle with a tablespoonful of lard, when brown throw in the meat cut into two inch squares; sprinkle over with a small handful of flour, pepper and salt and parsley chopped fine; keep stirring; the fire must not be too hot. A small piece of garlic chopped fine will give flavor without being disagreeable. When the meat is well moistened add some tomatoes peeled and seeded and cut in small squares. Pour over a half-glass of wine or stock; let all this simmer two and one-half or three hours. Carrots or turnips may be substituted for tomatoes.

VEAL.

Roast Loin of Veal.

Leave the kidney in the piece of veal; put plenty of salt around it, make a dressing the same as for chicken, and stuff around the kidney, and in the loin, put in the pan, with the thick side down, and roast in a hot oven, add hot water, in half an hour, and baste frequently; turn the roast, after the top side is done, and sprinkle a little flour on it, and baste again with melted butter.

For the gravy, stir in flour, and add a little hot water if necessary, and send to the table in a gravy boat.

Roast Fillet of Veal.

Pick out the fillet, take out the bone, and fill that place with stuffing, tie it up with a string to keep the stuffing in, and cook slowly at first, and baste with butter. Roast about three hours, according to the size.

Veal should always be washed carefully in cold water before cooking, and wiped dry on a clean cloth. Cold fillet of veal makes a nice stew.

Veal Loaf.

Three pounds of leg or loin of veal and one half pound salt pork, chopped finely together. Roll a dozen crackers, put half of them in the veal with two eggs, season with salt, and pepper, mix all together into a solid form, then take the crackers that are left, and spread smoothly on the outside. Bake one hour, and eat cold.

Veal Loaf No. 2.

Take three and one-half pounds of the finest part of the lean, and fat of a leg of veal chopped very fine, three common sized crackers rolled fine, two eggs, a piece of butter the size of an egg, a teaspoonful of salt, same of pepper, and a thick slice of pork chopped fine; mix all together, bake in a tin bread pan, put bits of butter and grated bread crumbs over it, and bake two hours, put a little water in another pan, and set this in, bake slowly. It should be eaten cold; cut in thin slices.

Veal Cutlets in Sour Cream.

Dry the slices of veal in a cloth, then dip in egg, and in cracker or bread crumbs; have ready a hot buttered spider into which put your veal; salt and pepper to taste. Pour over a cup of sour cream to each pound of meat, cover closely, until brown on one side, then turn, brown on the other, and serve immediately on hot platter.

Fried Veal Cutlets.

Have your lard or drippings very hot, then lay in the cutlet, seasoned with salt and pepper, and dredged with flour, brown nicely on both sides, cooking slowly until brown, lay the meat on your platter, and thicken the gravy with flour and drop an egg into it, stirring it quickly, then pour this dressing over the cutlets.

Fried Veal Chops.

Have your lard or drippings very hot, then put your chops in the pan, having first seasoned them well, and dipped them in egg and rolled in cracker crumbs. When a nice brown take out of the pan, lay on the platter, and add milk, flour, salt, and pepper, let it boil up, and serve hot in a separate dish.

Veal Turn-Over.

Mince fine, and season cold veal, two or three eggs, one cup of milk, flour to make good batter, (about five tablespoonfuls), heat one and one-half tablespoonfuls butter in skillet; mix parsley, pepper, and salt in batter to pour in skillet. As soon as it forms pour in meat; turn corners to make the turn-over in skillet, and when thoroughly cooked, slide upon a hot platter.

Veal Collops.

Cut veal in pieces size of an oyster, dip in egg, and roll in cracker crumbs, season with salt and pepper. Fry as you do oysters in hot lard or butter.

Veal Stew.

Cut the veal in small pieces, put on to cook with salt and pepper, and plenty of water; when done, make dumplings, the same as for stewed chicken, and put in the pot; cover tightly for fifteen minutes, then lay all on a platter; add a little butter and flour to the gravy, let it boil up once, then pour over the veal on the dish.

Veal Pot Pie.

Obtain veal cut from the breast or shoulder and cut in small pieces; wash and put in enough water to nearly cover; let it come to a boil and skim; season with salt, pepper and butter about the size of an egg, let it stew nearly an hour; for the crust, sift one pint flour with one heaping teaspoonful Gillett's Cream Tartar Baking Powder and a pinch of salt; mix it with one tablespoonful butter and enough milk to make a dough like biscuit; roll out about one inch thick, cut an opening in the centre, lay it on the meat, cover and boil twenty minutes; remove pot pie and meat and thicken the gravy with flour; add more water and butter if necessary.

Sweetbreads.

There are two sweetbreads in a calf that are very nice; put them in lukewarm water, the first thing, for a half hour, then throw into boiling hot water to whiten; take off the skin and they are ready to be cooked

Fried Sweetbreads.

Prepare as in the preceding recipe, then dip in egg, roll in cracker crumbs, season well and fry in hot lard.

MUTTON.

Roast Mutton.

The loin or leg is the best for roasting; wash thoroughly and wipe dry; put in the dripping pan with a little water to baste with, adding the salt after it has begun to roast, as it is apt to draw out too much blood and make it tough, if put on at first; baste frequently, and just before taking it up, sprinkle a little flour over it and baste with melted butter; skim the fat off the gravy and thicken with browned flour; allow about twelve minutes to the pound for roasting.

Boiled Leg of Mutton.

Wash the leg carefully and wipe dry on a cloth; put in a pot of hot salted water and boil until tender; skim off the fat occasionally; when tender lay on the platter and serve with drawn butter and one cup of capers or nasturtiums in it; allow twelve minutes to the pound for boiling.

Broiled Mutton Chops.

The loin is the part from which the chops are taken; place them on a buttered gridiron and broil over a nice hot fire; turn, and when broiled, season well with pepper, salt and melted butter.

Fried Mutton Chops.

Have some chops without much fat, dip them in egg, roll them in cracker crumbs, and fry them in hot lard and butter mixed; for the gravy, mix one tablespoonful of flour in a little cold water until free from lumps, stir into the gravy and pour over the chops, or serve with tomato sauce.

Roast Lamb.

Prepare the lamb same as the mutton; put in a dripping pan with a little water and let it roast slowly at first; then add more water, some salt, dredge with flour and baste. It will take about two hours to roast, and wants to be basted frequently. Mix a little flour and water together and add to the gravy Serve green peas and mint sauce with the roast lamb.

PORK.

Roast Loin of Pork.

Place the pork in the pan with a very little water under it; cook slowly at first, as the heat hardens the rind first; when done mix a little flour and water together and add to the gravy; serve with apple sauce. Some prefer stuffing with roast pork, and it may be made of bread crumbs, onion, a little sage, pepper and salt, and instead of roasting with the pork, may be baked on a separate dish.

Fried Pork Chops.

The pork chops are fried the same as mutton chops, and some people sprinkle a little powdered sage over them, also salt and pepper; then add a little flour to the gravy and pour over them; fried apples are delicious served with the fried pork chops, also tomato sauce.

Roast Spare Ribs.

Crack the ribs in the middle, sprinkle with salt and pepper, and put in the pan with a little water; when brown, turn on the other side until done.

Pork Tenderloins.

Chop the tenderloins in small pieces and fry a rich brown, in part butter and part lard; keep hot while making the gravy, and add a little flour to it, also a little Worcestershire sauce and pour over it.

Pork and Beans Baked.

Look over two quarts of beans, soak them over night in cold water; in the morning rinse in fresh water, parboil them a few minutes, then drain; add fresh water, a piece of salt pork, slit down the rind; when soft, add one tablespoonful of molasses and a little soda, stir well, then put in a tin pan and bake about two hours.

Fried Salt Pork.

Cut in slices, lay in cold water, then wipe dry; dust with flour and fry crisp; drain most of the grease from the frying pan, add some milk, pepper, salt and a tablespoonful of flour; stir until smooth; when finished, pour over the pork.

Fried Ham and Eggs.

Put a slice of ham in a hot spider and fry, turning quickly, until both sides are browned nicely; break each egg separately in a saucer and slip into the frying pan, into the ham fat; pour the hot fat over them, and as soon as the color changes, they are done; place them on top of the ham and send to the table hot.

Bacon and Eggs.

Fry lean strips of bacon until it is crisp, then take them out and lay on a platter; break the eggs separately, gently slide them into the bacon fat, and when they have set, turn the hot lard over them until they are done.

Roast Ham.

Boil the ham whole, and when it is done, let it lie in the water until cold; then skin it, put in a pan, roll in egg and bread crumbs, and put in the oven to roast; when done, put on a platter and serve cold.

Boiled Ham.

Wash the ham thoroughly, put it on the stove in a kettle of cold water and let it come to a boil, then keep it boiling steadily until done; allow about twenty minutes to the pound; if it is to be served hot, peel off the skin and stick in a few whole cloves; if the ham is to be served cold, let it stand in the pot until the water becomes cold, then peel off and serve the same.

Broiled Ham.

Place on the broiler and have a nice bed of coals to broil it; turn the slices frequently, and when it is done, put on a hot platter and pour melted butter over it. Some prefer to use boiled ham for broiling, instead of raw.

Potted Ham.

Chop the cold ham fine; season with pepper, salt, a little mustard and a pinch of mace; mix all together and put in the oven a half hour, then in a stone jar; cover the top with warm butter and tie them up.

French Sausage.

Mix one and a half pounds of lean pork with a half pound of fat, a little salt, pepper, one teaspoonful powdered sage, a little allspice and cloves; chop the meat fine, mix it all well together and pack it in a stone jar, and keep it in a cool place; when it is to be used, mold into cakes and fry in hot lard.

Boston Baked Beans.

Soak one quart of beans over night, in two quarts of cold water; in the morning turn off the water, add fresh water, and boil them until the membrane begins to separate, then turn off the water; put the beans in a baking pot, with a half pound of salt pork buried in the beans; add two tablespoonfuls of molasses and cover the whole with water; bake in a slow oven all day; watch the beans, and if they become dry, add more water; when thoroughly cooked, it will be known by the softness of the beans in the mouth, between the teeth and by the taste.

Dumpling for Pot Pie.

One pint flour, pinch of salt, heaping teaspoonful Gillet's Cream Tartar Baking Powder, one-half cup sweet milk; roll, cut in small biscuit shape, steam twenty minutes.

Meat Pie.

First prepare what cold meat you wish to use by cutting it up in small square pieces. Put in a kettle and boil in water until it is perfectly tender, then add flour to make gravy enough to fill the dish you wish to bake the pie in; salt and pepper to taste. For crust take one pint of flour, rub in about two tablespoonful of butter or lard, mix it thoroughly with the flour then add one teaspoonful of Gillett's Baking Powder (mix with water or milk); roll it out, then spread it over with enough butter to grease it; then sprinkle flour over it and roll again; take one half for bottom liner and the other half for top covering; put in oven and bake for about thirty or forty minutes.

POULTRY AND GAME.

Poultry and Game.

In picking out poultry select plump fat ones, being careful to see that they are fresh; and by trying the skin back of the wing you can tell if it is young and tender. With a turkey you can tell by rubbing the skin away from the breast bone, if that is easily broken it is sure to be young. Full grown poultry has the best flavor and are good for roasting, stewing and salads; the older ones may be made into soups, while spring chickens should either be broiled or fried. After a fowl has been cleaned and drawn it should be hung up for at least twenty-four hours and it will not hurt poultry to let it freeze, allowing it several hours in a warm room to thaw.

Pressed Chicken.

Boil a chicken in as little water as possible until the bones can be easily separated from the meat; remove all the skin, cut up and mix together the light and the dark meat; season with salt and pepper. Boil down the liquid in which the chicken was boiled, then pour it on the meat. Shape it like a loaf of bread; wrap tightly in a cloth and press a heavy weight on it for a few hours. Cut into slices and serve with parsley around it.

Fried Chicken.

Wash well; then cut up and wipe dry, season with pepper and salt, dip in flour or egg and roll in bread crumbs. Have a pan ready with butter and lard mixed; place the chicken in it and fry brown on both sides. This takes a little time as it wants to be cooked slowly. When fried put on a hot platter then add a tablespoonful of flour to the gravy; also a cup of sweet milk, salt and pepper, a little parsley; let it come to a boil, then pour over the chicken and serve hot.

Broiled Chicken.

Wash and dress the chicken well, as previously explained, and then split down the back, flatten the wings and breast bone without breaking it. Season with pepper and salt; place on the broiler having the inside to the fire, cover with a tin pan and let it broil slowly. It is a long job to broil a chicken nicely and usually takes half an hour. When it is broiled have a platter ready with some toast and melted butter, place the chicken on the toast and pour the butter over it. Garnish with sprigs of parsley.

Boiled Chicken.

Clean the same as for roasting; fill with an oyster dressing and sew a floured cloth around it, then put in a pot of boiling water. Let it boil for two hours and serve with oyster sauce.

Roast Chicken.

Clean carefully, singe and wipe with a damp cloth; stuff with a plain stuffing, with sage. Lay in a dripping pan with a teacupful of hot water, a small piece of butter, salt and pepper. Baste often and turn when one side becomes a nice brown. Dredge lightly with flour when nearly done and baste again with a little melted butter and the water in the pan. Put the giblets in the pan with the chicken and roast them. Thicken the gravy with a little flour and serve cranberry sauce with it.

Baked Chicken Pie.

Make a puff paste and line the sides and bottom of a baking dish, saving enough for the top. Cut up the chicken and fill the inside; season well with pepper, salt, butter and a sprinkling of flour, then put on the upper crust and bake slowly.

Chicken Fricassee.

Prepare the same as for roasting, then cut up two small chickens, put in a porcelain lined kettle and put in enough water to cover them. Let them cook for about an hour, or until tender. When finished add pepper, salt and butter, dissolve a tablespoonful of flour in a little water and add to the gravy. Let it boil up once, put the chicken on a hot platter, pour some of the gravy over it and put the rest in a gravy dish.

Chicken Pot Pie.

Cut up the chicken and boil in a pot till done; season with pepper, salt and a little butter and thicken with a little flour. Then add the dumplings, cook for fifteen minutes, being careful to have the top covered all the time to keep the dumplings from getting tough or heavy.

Jellied Chicken.

One good sized chicken boiled until tender; take out and save liquor. Pick up in small pieces; add to liquor, one box gelatine, salt and pepper, and small pieces of butter. Put all back in kettle, boil a few minutes, then pour in mold to get cold.

Stuffing for Chicken, Duck or Turkey.

Cook gizzard, liver and heart until tender, chop fine with one small onion; soak bread in the liquor that liver, etc. has been cooked in; season with salt and pepper to taste, add a little butter. Sage may used instead of onion.

Prairie Chicken, Roasted.

The chicken should not be too fresh; do not wash them; put plenty of butter inside each chicken, this is necessary to keep them moist. Roast half an hour or longer, if liked thoroughly done; baste them constantly with butter, when nearly done sprinkle over a little flour and plenty of butter to froth them. Serve on toast with water cresses around.

Broiled Pheasants.

Wash carefully, split down the back, wipe with a damp towel and broil same as quail. Pour melted butter over them after finished and serve on toast. Currant jelly is to be served with them.

Broiled Partridges.

Prepare the same as a pheasant; wipe with a towel and flatten on a broiler. When partly done season with pepper and salt and have hot melted butter ready to pour over them; place on squares of buttered toast. Serve currant jelly with them.

Broiled Squabs.

Prepare them the same as a spring chicken; split down the back, flatten the breast, wipe inside and out with a damp cloth. Put on a broiler, season with pepper and salt and when nicely broiled, pour melted butter over them. Serve on toast.

Broiled Quail on Toast.

Split down the back, clean and wipe carefully; place on a broiler and season with pepper and salt; when partly done cover with melted butter and serve on squares of toast. This is to be eaten with currant jelly.

Roasted Quails.

Cover the breasts with very thin slices of bacon, or rub them well with butter; roast, basting them often with butter. Fifteen or twenty minutes will cook sufficiently; salt and pepper to taste. Serve on a hot dish; bread sauce can be served with them.

Stewed Pigeons.

Tie them in shape; place pieces of bacon at the bottom of the stew pan, lay in the pigeons side by side, add a sliced carrot, an onion with a clove stuck in, a teaspoonful of sugar and some parsley; pour over enough water to cover them; put some thin slices of bacon over the top of each; pour boiling water when necessary; let them simmer until very tender.

How to Cook Duck.

To remove the fishy flavor put a carrot in each duck, put into boiling water, boil ten minutes then remove from the water and prepare with the usual dressing; then make a dough of flour and water, stiff enough to roll, roll half an inch thick; cover each duck after it is in a dripping pan; put in a little water. Bake the usual length of time, remove the dough when done and they will be moist and tender. No basting is required.

Wild Ducks.

Wild ducks should be cooked rare, with or without stuffing; baste them a few minutes at first with hot water to which has been added an onion and salt;

then take away the pan and baste with butter and a little flour to froth and brown them. The fire should be quite hot and twenty to thirty minutes is considered the outside limit for cooking them. A brown gravy made with the giblets should be served in the bottom of the dish. Serve also a currant jelly. Garnish the dish with slices of lemon.

Roast Wild Duck.

Wild duck may be kept several days in cold weather and it improves the flavor and quality very much.

Prepare the same as chicken, washing well and singeing; wipe carefully and if the ducks have any strong, fishy odor, put a cranberry or two inside them or rub a piece of onion over the breast. Put in a pan with a little water and some salt and baste quite often with melted butter. Turn and when a nice brown they are ready to serve. Wild ducks are not usually stuffed, though some prefer tomato dressing.

Roast Duck (Tame).

Clean thoroughly same as for other roast fowl and wipe carefully; beat the breast bone flat with a rolling pin, tie the wings and legs securely and stuff. Take one quart of bread crumbs and one onion chopped fine, a piece of butter, pepper, salt and a half teaspoonful of sage. After stuffing the duck sew it up nicely, to keep the flavor in; put in a dripping pan with a little water and baste often with salt water, turn so that the sides and back will be well browned. Prepare the giblets for the gravy same as in other roast fowl recipes and serve with currant jelly.

Roast Goose.

Prepare the goose the same as turkey, then if it is old parboil it about two hours. Fill it with an onion stuffing and sew the openings up carefully.

The stuffing is made as follows: two cups of stale bread crumbs, a chopped onion, little sage, pepper and salt, the yolk of one egg and a piece of butter. Place in a pan with a very little water and baste very frequently with salt and water. Bake about two hours, then take the gravy, add the giblets, chopped and the water they have been boiled in, thicken with a little flour and butter rubbed together and serve with apple sauce.

Boiled Turkey.

Prepare the same as for roast turkey and fill with an oyster stuffing and sew up with a white thread; tie the wings and legs close to the body and put in a kettle of boiling hot, salted water, being careful to have the breast downward. Boil until the skin breaks and skim frequently; serve with an oyster sauce. The liquid from this turkey makes delicious soup by seasoning same as chicken soup.

Roast Turkey.

Look over your turkey carefully, pluck the remaining feathers, singe thoroughly with paper, then draw it, preserving the liver, heart and gizzard. In separating the liver be very careful not to break the gall-bag, as it renders the turkey uneatable if broken, by making it very bitter, it being impossible to remove the taste by washing. Have ready a filling of oysters, bread crumbs, sweet marjoram, parsley, salt, pepper and butter; fill the body and breast of the turkey with this mixture and then sew up with a thread and tie the legs. Dredge lightly with flour; baste frequently with a little melted butter and when one side is nicely browned turn and brown the other. Chop the liver, heart and gizzard fine and add them to the gravy, thicken with a tablespoonful of flour, dissolved in a little water and place in a gravy tureen. Serve with cranberry sauce.

SAUCES.

Bread Sauce.

One cup of stale bread crumbs, one small onion, pinch of salt, little pepper, piece of butter size of egg, little mace and a bay leaf. Cook the onion in two cups of milk until soft, then pour over the stale bread crumbs, after having been strained; then add the bay leaf, mace, onions, pepper and salt, and boil and stir continually; serve in a boat.

Brown Sauce.

Take one pint of stock and pour it over two tablespoonfuls butter and two tablespoonfuls flour, which has been melted and mixed well together; stir well and add a pinch of salt, pepper and a little onion juice, and serve. You may brown the butter and flour first if preferred, and then add the stock, etc., afterwards.

Fish Sauce.

To a drawn butter add one tablespoonful Worcestershire sauce, pinch of salt and four hard-boiled eggs chopped fine; serve with boiled fish, and garnish with sliced lemon and parsley.

Anchovy Sauce.

To a drawn butter add two teaspoonfuls anchovy paste and one teaspoonful onion juice. This is for boiled or fried fish, and the anchovy paste can be procured from your grocer, in bottles.

Maitre d' Hotel Sauce.

To a half pint of drawn butter add the juice of a lemon, one tablespoonful of onion, chopped fine, one and one-half tablespoonfuls chopped parsley, one tablespoonful lemon juice, half a teaspoonful powdered summer savory, pinch of salt and cayenne pepper. Cook well and serve with any kind of salt fish, broiled or fried.

Curry Sauce.

Make a drawn butter sauce (given elsewhere), add one large slice of onion, pounded, and a teaspoonful of curry powder; serve with saute of meat or fish.

Currant Jelly Sauce.

Two tablespoonfuls butter, one-half onion, one bay leaf, one tablespoonful of flour, half a teacupful of currant jelly, one and one-half tablespoonfuls vinegar, a little celery, salt, pepper and a cup of strong stock. Cook the butter and flour until smooth, add the onion, bay leaf, celery, vinegar, salt and pepper; when brown add the stock and let simmer slowly for fifteen minutes; strain through a sieve, add the jelly, stir until it is all melted, and serve with game.

Hollandaise Sauce.

Make a drawn butter, beat in gradually the yolks of two eggs, one by one, the juice of half a lemon, a speck of cayenne pepper, a pinch of salt, a little chopped parsley and a trifle of onion juice; beat well with an egg-beater until frothy. This is served with baked fish and croquettes.

Mushroom Sauce.

Cook one tablespoonful of butter and one teaspoonful of flour in a sauce pan; when smooth, stir in one cup of stock, one-half cup of canned mushroom liquor; let it simmer, then strain; add one can French mushrooms, salt, pepper, and a little lemon juice squeezed in; serve while hot.

Mushroom Sauce No. 2.

Two tablespoonfuls of butter browned, one tablespoonful of flour stirred into it; put in can of mushroom liquor and mushrooms quartered. If too thick stir in a little hot water; add lastly one tablespoonful Worcestershire sauce.

Parsley Sauce.

To a drawn butter sauce add two tablespoonfuls parsley. This may be colored with spinach, and served with fish chiefly.

Tomato Sauce.

Put one-half dozen tomatoes, one bay leaf, a sprig of parsley, some pepper and salt through a hair sieve; after it is well strained, put some butter the size of an egg into a sauce-pan, after it is melted add a teaspoonful of flour; stir well; after it has cooked thoroughly add the tomato pulp and stir until smooth.

Excellent Cream Sauce.

FOR POTATOES, OYSTERS, ETC.

Two tablespoonfuls of butter (heat, but do not brown), two heaping teaspoonfuls flour; stir in the hot butter until smooth, add pint of milk gradually; salt, etc.

Caper Sauce.

Make a drawn butter sauce and add a half cup of French capers; beat in the yolk of one egg and the juice of one lemon.

Mint Sauce.

Chop one bunch of mint fine; put in a boat and add two tablespoonfuls sugar, vinegar enough to cover, and let stand an hour before serving.

Oyster Sauce.

Take a half dozen large oysters to every pound of fish and let them scald in a half pint of their own liquor, then remove the oysters, season the liquor with a little salt, pepper, butter and a pinch of mace; then add one teaspoonful of flour dissolved in a little cold milk; cook a moment, add the oysters and serve in a gravy boat. You may chop the oysters or not, as you wish.

Cream Sauce.

Scald one cup of milk, add pepper, salt, chopped parsley and a piece of butter, then stir into this one teaspoonful of corn starch dissolved in cold water: beat one egg very lightly, then beat the mixture into it, set on the stove a moment, then pour on the fish or serve in a boat.

Egg Sauce.

Mix half a cup of flour with half a cup of warm butter; then have a farina boiler ready with a pint of milk and a little salt and pepper; let it boil, then stir in the butter and flour, and stir rapidly until it becomes creamy. Chop fine three hard-boiled eggs and add to the sauce, beating them thoroughly, and serve in a boat. You can substitute cream for butter, and by leaving out the eggs you have a very good white sauce.

Drawn Butter.

Butter melted is used with all kinds of fish, and requires skill to make it nicely, put a cup of butter in a pan with a tablespoonful of flour, mix well and add a half cup of warm water; cover up the pan and let it simmer slowly until it begins to boil; then it is ready for use. In melting butter for pudding sauce, substitute milk for water.

Chili Sauce.

Thirty-four large tomatoes, seven green peppers, seven onions, seven tablespoonfuls sugar, seven tablespoonfuls salt, seven cups of vinegar. Boil tomatoes and onions together until soft, add peppers, etc., boil down to one gallon.

India Sauce.

Two dozen tomatoes, twelve apples, one-half gallon vinegar, one pound brown sugar, one pound raisins (chopped fine), one-half pound salt, one large red pepper, six or eight onions, boil one hour, then put through a coarse sieve or colander, add one-quarter pound ginger, one-quarter pound mustard mixed with a little cold vinegar; boil one-half hour. When cold, bottle and cork tight.

Mrs. Drake's Cranberry Sauce.

One quart of cranberries, two teacupfuls of sugar, one teacupful of hot water. Put the water in a porcelain lined kettle, then put in the sugar and let it dissolve. Wash the cranberries and drain through a colander; boil the syrup a minute, then put in the cranberries and boil ten minutes, stirring all the time; take care or they will burn. Pour into molds and let them stand until cold and hard. This is the only way to cook cranberries to prevent the skins from being hard.

Apple Sauce.

Pare and quarter the apples, put them in a porcelain kettle with a little water; boil until tender, then put in sugar to suit the taste; boil a few minutes longer; use only sour, juicy apples. To be eaten cold.

Apple Sauce No. 2.

To make sauce of apples that are neither sweet nor sour and of an indifferent quality, take half a dozen apples, one teacupful of sugar, one teacupful of water and one lemon. Pare, core and quarter the apples, put them in a porcelain kettle with the sugar and water; stew slowly; when done add the lemon.

Stewed Dried Fruit.

All kinds of dried fruit should be carefully looked over, thoroughly washed and drained in a colander. It should then be soaked an hour or more before boiling; put it over in a porcelain lined kettle and boil until nearly done, then add the sugar to taste and cook until soft. Many kinds of dried fruit such as apricots, peaches, etc., can be soaked and then cooked in a syrup, the same as fresh fruit, making a nice preserve almost equal to preserves made from fresh ripe fruit

To Brown Flour.

Spread flour on a tin and stir continually until it becomes brown all over. It is excellent for coloring brown sauces and thickening many dishes.

To Brown Butter.

Take a piece of butter the size of an egg, stir it until it begins to brown, then stir in a little brown flour until smooth. This is used to color gravies and meats.

Vinagrette Sauce.

One teaspoonful of white pepper, one teaspoonful salt, one and one-half teaspoonfuls mustard, one and one-half cupfuls vinegar, one teaspoonful of oil; mix salt, pepper and mustard together, then very slowly add the vinegar and after mixing well, add the oil. This sauce is to be eaten on cold meats or on cold fish.

Celery Sauce.

Boil two heads of celery until tender; put through a sieve, add the well-beaten yolk of an egg with a little lemon juice, butter, salt and pepper to taste. This may be thickened with a little flour.

Oyster Sauce, For Turkey.

A pint of oysters cut up small and boiled in their own liquor; add a cup of cream, tablespoonful of flour made smooth with part of the cream, salt, pepper and butter

Sour Gravy.

One pint hot water, one-half cupful vinegar, one half cupful sugar, or to taste, one-half teaspoonful nutmeg and butter size of egg.

SALADS AND DRESSINGS.

To prevent eggs turning dark colored after being boiled for salad use, first put them into cold water. Boil 5 or 10 minutes slowly after the water begins to boil, then take out, and put in cold water a few minutes to cool.

Fish Salad.

Boil a fish (whitefish or trout) when done, take the bones out, cool, and cut to pieces; chop as much celery as you have fish, with butter and salt to taste; use any salad dressing.

Cucumber Salad.

Peel and slice cucumbers, mix with salt and let stand half an hour; mix two tablespoonfuls sweet oil, or ham gravy, with as much vinegar, and a tablespoonful sugar. Add the cucumbers, which should be drained a little; add a teaspoonful pepper and stir well; sliced onions are an addition if their flavor is liked.

Salmon Salad.

Yolks of two eggs well beaten, one teaspoonful pepper, one teaspoonful salt, one teaspoonful sugar, one and a half teaspoonfuls made mustard, one tablespoonful melted butter, four tablespoonfuls vinegar, one tablespoonful lemon juice, stir all together, set over kettle till it thickens, then put in a cool place. Before using, thin with cream; to one can of salmon (picked over carefully all bones, and skin thrown out) use six heads of celery, chopped fine.

Salmon Salad for Half Can.

Half can salmon, set in boiling water awhile, take out in dish, and pour off oil, take out bones and skin, cover with cold vinegar, salt and pepper, and let stand. Beat the yolk of one raw egg, mash fine the yolk of one hard-boiled egg, a little dry mustard, one and a half tablespoonfuls melted butter, vinegar, and lemon juice, (about half a lemon), *little* sugar, mix all together, then add half as much celery as salmon, mix lightly with a fork, serve on lettuce leaves. A little cream is nice, added the last thing to the dressing.

Chicken Salad.

Yolks of two eggs well beaten, one teaspoonful salt, one teaspoonful pepper, two teaspoonfuls of white sugar, two teaspoonfuls made mustard, one tablespoonful butter, little lemon juice; stir into this mixture four tablespoonfuls best vinegar; cook over kettle; thin with cream; take one cup celery to one cup picked chicken, add one tablespoonful vinegar, juice of one-fourth of an onion, little pepper and salt, and let stand; when ready for use, pour over the dressing, and serve on lettuce leaves; grate onion for juice.

Chicken Salad, No. 2.

Two cold fowls, remove the skin and fat, pick up very fine; two heads of celery, or four small ones, mix and set away; mix the yolks of nine hard-boiled eggs to a paste, mix with half pint of sweet cream, half cup of melted butter, eight teaspoonfuls mustard, one small teaspoonful cayenne pepper, one small teaspoonful salt, half-pint vinegar, mix all together, longer the better, five minutes before serving pour over the chicken and celery.

Cabbage Salad.

Two cups vinegar, one tablespoonful flour, two eggs, one teaspoonful mustard, a little pepper, salt, sugar, and butter size of an egg; chop the cabbage fine, then pour over it this dressing, after it has been cooked in a farina boiler, and set away to cool.

Potato Salad.

Six cold-boiled potatoes, one medium sized onion, sliced thin, lay in a dish, first a layer of potato, then onion, till the dish is full; sprinkle with pepper and salt, also on top, add four tablespoonfuls of sweet cream, melt one-half cup of butter, with half a pint of vinegar, when it is boiling hot pour over the salad, and serve.

Beet Salad.

Chop beets and celery fine and set away; yolks of two eggs well beaten, one teaspoonful salt, one teaspoonful pepper, two teaspoonfuls white sugar, two teaspoonfuls made mustard, one tablespoonful butter, little lime juice; stir into this mixture four tablespoonfuls best vinegar, cook over kettle, stir till it thickens; if necessary, thin with cream, before adding to the beets and celery.

Tomato Salad.

One head lettuce, six large ripe tomatoes, half-cup of mayonnaise; peel the tomatoes, and set on ice, wash and dry the lettuce, cut the tomatoes in halves, and lay on the lettuce, and pour over the mayonnaise.

Summer Salad.

Four or five firm ripe tomatoes, three small cucumbers, two small onions, cut the tomatoes about the size of dice, chop the onions (not very fine), cut up the cucumber, salt and pepper, and serve on a lettuce leaf with the following dressing:—one egg, one teaspoonful salt, one and a half teaspoonfuls sugar, one teaspoonful white pepper, mix all together, then slowly add three tablespoonfuls of fresh salad oil, stirring constantly; when thoroughly mixed add one tablespoonful sweet cream, and one tablespoonful of lemon juice, or vinegar.

Lobster Salad.

One can lobster, two head celery, half-pint of mayonnaise; pick the lobster fine, chop the celery and mix thoroughly, pour over the dressing, and serve on a lettuce leaf, garnish with a chain of the whites of hard-boiled eggs, and grate the yolks fine, and sprinkle on top.

Shrimp Salad.

One can shrimps, half-pint of mayonnaise, remove the shrimps from the can, wash in cold water, dry in a napkin, then mix well with the mayonnaise, serve on a lettuce leaf. Sardines may be fixed the same way.

Lettuce Salad.

Wash the crisp centre leaves of lettuce, dry carefully, tear apart and cover with a French dressing, and serve; nasturtiums and water-cress may be used in the same way.

Fruit Salad.

Six oranges, six bananas, white grapes, sliced peaches, cocoanut grated, and other fruits that are in season: four tablespoonfuls white sugar, one cup of sherry, two tablespoonfuls of Madeira, one-half teaspoonful cinnamon; mix sugar and cinnamon, add the other ingredients, stir thoroughly till the sugar is dissolved, then pour over the fruit.

Mustard Dressing.

Yolks of six eggs, five teaspoonfuls of white sugar, five teaspoonfuls of mustard, one teaspoonful salt; beat all well together, then drop in olive oil until it becomes quite stiff; boil one pint of cider vinegar and stir in gradually, heat and mix thoroughly.

Simple Mustard Dressing.

One tablespoonful mustard, two teaspoonfuls butter, two teaspoonfuls sugar, two teaspoonfuls corn starch, half teaspoonful salt, pinch of pepper, mix all together to a smooth paste, then stir in one cup of cider vinegar and boil two or three minutes, stirring all the time; this is nice for chopped cabbage or lettuce.

Mrs. Drake's Salad Dressing.

Yolks of four eggs, two teaspoonfuls sugar, one teaspoonful of mustard, half teaspoonful of salt, mix all together, and with a fork stir in salad oil until it becomes quite stiff; then add three tablespoonfuls of cream; boil one pint of vinegar, and stir it into the mixture a little at a time until thoroughly mixed.

Simple Salad Dressing.

One egg, one teaspoonful butter, one teaspoonful sugar, half teaspoonful mustard, salt and pepper to taste; beat the eggs, melt the butter, and mix all together with two tablespoonfuls of cold vinegar; boil a small teacupful of vinegar, and stir it slowly into the mixture, being careful that it does not curdle;

set on the stove, and boil a minute stirring all the time; this dressing can be made in two or three minutes, and is very good for potato salad, lettuce, or any other simple salad.

Salad Dressing.

Three eggs, quarter teacupful of butter, one teaspoonful mustard, wet with a little vinegar, then fill the cup two-thirds full, also half teacupful of sweet milk. season to taste, with black and red pepper, little sugar; add whites of eggs beaten stiff, and cook with the rest; when cold, add one teacupful of sweet or sour cream; this is very nice for either salmon or cabbage.

Salad Dressing without Oil.

Two tablespoonfuls vinegar, two tablespoonfuls corn starch; a little pepper, (cayenne), one teaspoonful salt, one teacupful milk, yolks of three eggs, small piece of butter; boil the milk, wet the corn starch in a little cold milk, add to the hot milk, until it thickens; then add the yolks of the eggs well beaten, let it cook, remove from fire and add salt, pepper, butter, and vinegar, let cool.

Dressing.

For lettuce, tomatoes, cabbage, or cold potatoes if sliced and sprinkled with vinegar awhile before, the following dressing is excellent:—one tablespoonful butter, one egg beaten to a cream, one teaspoonful salt, half teaspoonful of mustard, two-thirds of a cup of vinegar; put all in porcelain kettle; stir till as thick as rich cream, remove from stove; when cold is ready for use.

Dressing for Cabbage.

Rub two tablespoonfuls butter with one tablespoonful flour, then add one egg, put on the stove and let cook; then add four tablespoonfuls vinegar, pepper, salt, and mustard: when ready for use, add one teacupful of thick sour cream, and lastly a little more vinegar.

French Dressing.

Three tablespoonfuls olive oil, one tablespoonful vinegar, half teaspoonful salt, quarter teaspoonful black or cayenne pepper; put the salt and pepper in a bowl, then add the oil, drop by drop, beating hard, until the salt is dissolved, then add the vinegar slowly; then stir for a few minutes thoroughly, and set away.

Mayonnaise Dressing.

Yolk of one egg, half teaspoonful raw mustard, half teaspoonful salt, half teaspoonful cayenne pepper, one and a half teaspoonfuls vinegar; mix thoroughly till perfectly smooth, then add half pint olive oil, drop by drop; this will make a thick batter, and can be thinned with cream, or vinegar, and will suffice for a pound of salad.

Cream Salad Dressing.

Yolks of eight eggs, half teaspoonful mustard, two tablespoonfuls vinegar, juice of one lemon, one pint of cream, little celery salt; put in a saucepan, let boil stirring the cream in slowly, before it is hot.

Mustard.

One teaspoonful vinegar, one-half teacupful mustard, mix together, and place on the fire, add one teaspoonful sugar, half teaspoonful salt, and pepper, one teaspoonful butter, stir until thick; put an onion sliced, in the vinegar the night before; when ready to make, take out the onions.

Dressing for Ham Sandwiches.

Yolks of eight eggs, one teacupful of vinegar, one tablespoonful mustard, salt and pepper to taste. Boil the vinegar, then add eggs, salt and pepper. Boil till thick; when cold, add the mustard mixed with the ham, chopped fine.

ENTREES.

Calves' Brains.

Soak the brains in salt water for several hours; pick off all the skin after soaking; then stew them a few minutes in some salted water, turning them once; take them out and while they are cooling roll several crackers to a powder and beat an egg; then take the brains and slice them as thin as possible; dip them first in the eggs then in the cracker dust and have a pan of hot butter with a little lard mixed to keep it from scorching, and fry the brains to a beautiful brown. Serve while hot.

Sweet Breads.

Put in salt water for one hour; then put in boiling water for twenty minutes; then roll in cracker crumbs and fry in lard and butter, one tablespoonful of each, or all butter.

Mock Smelts.

This is a fine dish which is not fish at all. Make noodle dough as for soup, beating together with a rolling pin three eggs, a teaspoonful of salt and flour to make a stiff dough; cut into four pieces, roll out as thin as paper, spread on a paper to dry and when dry enough roll up. With a sharp knife shave the roll into thin rings and boil them five minutes in water boiling when they are put in; brown a pint of bread crumbs in butter in a frying pan; skim out the mock smelts into the crumbs; pour a teacupful of milk over all; let it heat up then serve.

Little Pigs in Blankets.

Season large oysters with salt and pepper; cut fat bacon in very thin slices; wrap one oyster in each slice and fasten with toothpicks; heat frying pan and put in the little pigs; cook just long enough to crisp the bacon, about five minutes; place on slices of toast, cut small and serve immediately; do not remove the skins, garnish with parsley. This is a nice relish for lunch or tea.

Breakfast Relish or Oysters.

Fry one and a half dozen oysters a nice brown, and lay them on five or six slices of well-toasted bread. Over this sprinkle thickly fine cut celery; pour over a pint of hot milk, adding butter and salt; thicken with flour to the consistency of cream. Serve hot.

Salmon Loaf.

Two pounds salmon (canned), four eggs beaten well; chop a little parsley fine and stir into four tablespoonfuls of melted butter, salt, and red pepper to taste. Stir into this half teacupful of bread crumbs, then the eggs, and put all into the salmon; stir and steam one hour.

Sauce.—One teacupful of milk brought to a boiling point; then add one tablespoonful corn starch, one tablespoonful melted butter stirred into salmon liquor, one egg, stir into the mixture and cook; then add four teaspoonfuls of catsup.

Escalloped Ham.

Chop the ham after it has been boiled; make a cream sauce, pepper, salt (if the ham is not salt enough) lemon juice, parsley; boil some eggs hard, put through the ricer. Fill the dish with a layer of ham, then cream sauce, then eggs, cracker crumbs on top, with a little butter to brown nicely.

Escalloped Chicken.

Pick the meat from the bones of a cold chicken, remove skin and gristle, chop quite fine. In the bottom of a buttered dish, sprinkle a thick layer of cracker crumbs; make this very wet with milk, then put in a layer of meat, sprinkle salt, pepper, and quite large pieces of butter on this. If the chicken has been baked, add small pieces of the dressing, then another layer of cracker crumbs, and make them very wet with milk, and continue as before. After the last layer of meat, take the gravy; if boiled, put a little of the broth in the oven, brown, then pour in the rest of the broth, and thicken, if baked, warm with a little hot water, and pour over it. For the top, take cracker crumbs, very wet with warm milk, then beat two eggs well, and stir into the cracker crumbs; pepper, salt, and butter. When you put it in the oven, put plate on top, not large enough to cover it entirely. You will know when it is done, by its bubbling around the edge of the plate, Remove the plate and let brown.

Potted Beef.

Take a fore shank of beef, (have your butcher saw it instead of chopping to avoid small bones); put on the fire with enough cold water to cover it; let it boil until the meat falls off the bones; then 'take out, but save the water. Chop the meat into about half inch pieces; skim the boiled water and return the meat. Chop fine a good-sized onion, thyme, handful of parsley and a section of garlic. Toast a slice of bread, place in the oven till crisp, then roll fine. Cayenne pepper and salt to taste. Mix thoroughly with the meat and simmer for three or four hours, stirring; place in glasses or cups; put in cool place.

Rice Pone.

One pint of boiled rice, three eggs, one pint of fresh milk, two ounces of butter, one small teacupful of cornmeal, salt to taste; break eggs very light, add milk and rice, then melted butter, meal, salt and whites of eggs beaten to a froth; bake from one-half to three-quarters of an hour.

CROQUETTES.

Bean Croquettes.

Wash one pint of white beans, and let soak over night; in the morning drain, cover with cold water, let boil for one hour; when done, drain, put into a keystone egg beater, and whip till they are mashed fine; press through a colander, and set away; then add one tablespoonful molasses, one tablespoonful vinegar, one tablespoonful butter, one teaspoonful salt, a little white pepper, mix all thoroughly with the beans, and put away to cool; then form into balls, dip in beaten egg, roll in cracker dust, and fry in hot drippings.

Veal Croquettes.

Put on the stove in a saucepan two ounces of butter, in which fry, till slightly colored, one small onion; now add two coffee-cups of cold finely chopped veal (roast is best, but any other kind will do), a slice of bread first soaked in cold water and then squeezed as dry as possible, in a napkin; a little thyme, a tablespoonful of chopped parsley, a little grated nutmeg and lemon peel, salt, white and cayenne pepper to taste; when thoroughly heated, remove from the stove, and add three tablespoonfuls of cream or milk, and a well-beaten egg; mix all well, and heap in an earthen dish. When cold add another egg, two, if the mixture is at all dry, as it should be as moist, as you can work it; make in molds, dip in egg, roll in cracker dust, and fry in hot drippings; two minutes is long enough to brown them; one teacupful of boiled rice may be used instead of the bread, and will be a great addition to the croquettes.

Ham Croquettes.

One teacupful cooked ham chopped fine, two teacupfuls mashed potatoes, yolks of three eggs, one tablespoonful butter, cayenne to taste; mix potatoes, butter, yolks of two eggs and cayenne, beat until smooth, then set to cool; chop the ham, mix with the other yolk set on stove a moment, then turn out to cool, when thoroughly cool, take a tablespoonful of the potato mixture, make a hole, then put a large teaspoonful the ham inside, shape into a ball, like a potato; after dipping in egg, and rolling in crumbs (either bread or cracker) fry in boiling lard.

Sweetbread Croquettes.

Two sweetbreads, one teacupful cream, yolks of two eggs, one tablespoonful butter, one tablespoonful chopped parsley, two tablespoonfuls flour, half teaspoonful onion juice, quarter teaspoonful nutmeg, quarter teaspoonful white pepper; first throw the sweetbreads in cold water, then in boiling water, skin carefully. and cut with a silver knife; heat the cream, then rub the butter and flour smooth, and stir into the cream till thick; then set off the stove, add the yolks well-beaten, the sweetbreads, parsley, onion juice, nutmeg and pepper, salt to taste; put away to cool; then form into croquettes, dip in egg, roll in crumbs and fry in boiling fat; some use a half teacupful of chopped mushrooms with the mixture also.

Oyster Croquettes.

Two dozen oysters, one teacupful oyster liquor, one teacupful of cream, one tablespoonful chopped parsley, one tablespoonful of butter, two tablespoonfuls of flour, yolks of two eggs, cayenne pepper and salt, quarter of a nutmeg grated; boil the oysters in their own liquor, stir for five minutes, then drain; chop fine, then put a teacupful of this liquor and the cream in a saucepan, rub the flour and butter smooth, add this and the chopped oysters to the boiling liquor and cream, stir till it thickens, add the yolks of the eggs well beaten; stir well, then add parsley, salt, cayenne pepper and nutmeg; mix thoroughly, and set to cool; when cold, shape, and dip in egg, and roll in cracker or bread crumbs, and fry in boiling lard.

Shad Roe Croquettes.

Two shad roes, one teacupful sweet cream, yolks of two eggs, one tablespoonful butter, two tablespoonfuls flour, one teaspoonful lemon juice, one tablespoonful parsley chopped fine, quarter of a nutmeg grated, cayenne pepper and salt to taste; carefully wash the shad roes, then put them on the stove, in a saucepan of boiling water, add a teaspoonful of salt, cover and let simmer slowly a few minutes; then remove the skin and mash them; heat the cream, rub the butter and flour together, add to the cream while boiling, stir till thick; then add yolks, remove from the stove, add all other ingredients, thoroughly mix, and turn in an earthen dish to cool; when cold form into croquettes, cone shape, or rolls, dip in beaten egg, and roll in bread crumbs, and fry in boiling lard; serve with sauce Hollandaise.

Rice Croquettes.

One teacupful of cold boiled rice, half teacupful of sweet milk, one tablespoonful of sugar, one teaspoonful salt, a little lemon peel grated, one egg; let it get cold, then shape in oval balls; dip in egg, then in bread crumbs, or rolled crackers, and fry a rich brown in boiling lard.

Potato Croquettes.

Two teacupfuls mashed potatoes, half a teacupful hot cream or milk, one tablespoonful melted butter, a little nutmeg; whites of two eggs beaten well; beat the potatoes and hot milk together until very light, add the butter, nutmeg, and whites of eggs; form in cone shape, cover with beaten egg, roll in sifted crumbs; then fry in lard hot enough to brown quickly.

Chicken Croquettes.

One pint cold roast chicken chopped fine, one small onion, one large slice of bread, one tablespoonful butter, two eggs well beaten; put the butter on the stove in a saucepan, fry the onion in it, until slightly colored; now add the chopped chicken, the bread, (first soaked in cold water and pressed as dry as possible in a cloth), a little thyme, a tablespoonful of chopped parsley, a little grated nutmeg, and lemon peel, salt, white and cayenne pepper to taste; heat thoroughly then remove from the stove, and add three tablespoonfuls of milk or cream if you have it, and one egg; mix all thoroughly, and heap on an earthen dish; when cold add the other egg, two if the mixture is too dry to shape into rolls about two and a half inches long, and dip in beaten egg, and bread crumbs.

Salmon Croquettes.

Two teacupfuls cooked salmon, two teacupfuls mashed potatoes, one-quarter of a teaspoonful of curry powder, one cooking spoonful of butter, two tablespoonfuls of cream, salt and pepper to taste; remove all the bones from the salmon; chop very fine, and mix well together; if not thin enough, add a little more cream; shape into cones and fry quickly in boiling lard; the yolks of two hard-boiled eggs, and bread crumbs, may be used instead of potatoes and nutmeg and anchovy sauce, in the place of curry powder.

Beef Croquettes.

Two teacupfuls of cold roast beef chopped fine, one dozen oysters chopped, one teacupful bread crumbs, a little mustard, nutmeg, pepper and salt, one spoonful of butter, two spoonfuls of gravy, one egg; for croquettes and such dishes, do not beat the eggs enough to break the threads, always beat in the same direction; soak the bread crumbs in a little hot milk until soft, add mustard, grated nutmeg; pepper, salt, and butter melted in the hot milk, and gravy that is nearly always left over with the roast; stir in one beaten egg, at the last, and make into rolls like large corks, dip them into an egg beaten with one tablespoonful of cold water, and roll in fine bread crumbs; fry in hot drippings or butter.

Meat Croquettes.

Three teacupfuls cold meat, quarter loaf of bread, one desert spoonful parsley, three eggs; a pinch of ground mace or nutmeg; a desert spoonful of ground ginger, pepper and salt; any nice cold meat when finely minced will make good croquettes. Use a quarter of a loaf of bread well soaked in water, and squeezed dry, mix with the minced meat, chopped parsley, eggs, mace, ground ginger, pepper and salt; roll them into egg-shaped balls; have ready two or three well-beaten eggs in one plate, and flour or rolled cracker or bread crumbs in another; first roll in the flour, then in the egg, then again in the flour, and fry in boiling drippings; serve hot. If preferred a small onion and three tablespoonfuls of cream may be added to the croquettes, if made of veal; some prefer not to use ginger; a little thyme and grated lemon peel is good in beef croquettes.

PATTIES.

Chicken Patties.

Mince cold roasted or boiled chicken and season well; stir into this a sauce, made of one-half pint of milk into which, when boiling, a teaspoonful of corn starch has been added to thicken it; season with a teaspoonful of butter; salt and pepper. Line patty pans with a good puff paste, bake the crust in a brisk oven; then fill the pans and set in the oven a few minutes, to brown very slightly.

Chicken Patties No. 2.

One teacupful of cold roast or boiled chicken chopped fine, one tablespoonful of flour, one teacupful of chicken gravy, salt and pepper, a few green celery leaves. Cream, milk or hot water can be used instead of gravy, and a teaspoonful of corn starch instead of flour. A little mace, nutmeg or lemon peel may be used instead of the celery. Put into a sauce pan on the stove, add a cup of cold gravy; salt, white and cayenne pepper to taste. When hot add a tablespoonful of flour, rubbed smooth in a small quantity of butter; let simmer a few minutes; take from the fire and add quarter teacupful of sweet cream. Line some patty pans with puff paste and rub the the edge of the crust with butter to prevent the cover from sticking; put a round cracker in each patty pan; put on the top crust, rolled thin, and bake in a quick oven. When done remove the tops, take out the cracker, fill with the prepared chicken; put in oven a moment and serve hot.

Oyster Patties.

Three dozen large fresh oysters, three ounces of butter, a little mace pounded or ground, a bit of cayenne pepper, a little salt, two cooking spoonfuls of cream, a few green celery leaves. Take three dozen oysters, cut each into three or four pieces, and scald them in their own liquor. Put the butter in a saucepan, sift in sufficient flour to absorb the butter; strain the oyster liquor into the saucepan with the butter and flour; add the mace, celery, cayenne and salt to taste; let boil up, put in the oysters, add three tablespoonfuls cream, allow to heat, but do not boil. Line patty-pans with puff paste, and put into each a round cracker; cover with paste, and bake a light brown; when done remove the lids of the patty-dishes, take out the crackers, fill with the mixture, replace the covers, set in the oven for a moment and serve hot. The yolks of two large-boiled eggs mashed fine, may be used instead of the cream.

Beef of Veal Patties.

Boil meat, after it is cool, chop fine, take stock (left from the meat) and thicken with two tablespoonfuls flour, two or three tablespoonfuls cream, a little pepper and salt. After it comes to a boil, pour in the meat, keep hot, and pour into patty shells just before serving. Make the shells the same as in the recipe for oyster or chicken patties.

Sweetbread Patties.

Throw the sweetbreads in salt water one hour, then boil, and throw into ice water two or three times to blanch; then pick up fine. Boil mushrooms till tender, chop fine, mix equal amount of sweetbreads and mushrooms together, make a dressing, composed of sweet cream, two tablespoonfuls butter and add flour to make quite thick; add more cream, mix all well, and boil up once. Make the crust the same as for oyster or chicken patties.

EGGS AND OMELETTES.

Eggs are very nutritious, a dozen being equal to two pounds of beef steak. If properly cooked, they are the best and most easily digested food for invalids and delicate people. Raw eggs are very often given to those who cannot eat other solid food; there are so many ways of cooking eggs, that an almost endless variety of dishes can be prepared from them. Bread crumbs and dry bread can be used in preparing these delicate breakfast and lunch dishes; half a dozen eggs, half a loaf of bread or a cup of bread crumbs, a tomato or two, and a little butter properly put together, and you have a breakfast for a family of four; no one who properly understands how to use eggs, will ever be at a loss to prepare a meal; in beating eggs always beat one way; in making custards, pies, cakes or puddings, stir the mixture one way as much as possible, by doing this the grain of the egg is not broken and is much lighter. Limed eggs nearly always have a peculiar flavor that spoils them for most people.

Baked Eggs. No. 1.

Half-a-dozen eggs, lard or drippings, salt and pepper to taste. Six slices of buttered toast. Use patty pans or gem tins to bake the eggs in. Grease the tins and lay a little piece of butter in each, then break an egg in each tin, sprinkle over a little salt and pepper, and put in the oven to bake; as soon as they set put them on the oven grate a moment. Serve on well-buttered slices of toast; put a small piece of butter on each egg. This is a nicer way to cook eggs than to poach them.

Baked Eggs. No. 2.

Five eggs, a teacupful of bread crumbs, half a teacupful of milk, tablespoonful of butter, salt and pepper to taste. Pour the milk over the bread, mix the eggs, milk and bread together; add butter, pepper and salt. Grease a tin and pour the mixture in it, and place in a moderately hot oven. When done on the bottom put the tin on the grate of the oven for a minute or two. Serve on a hot platter, and garnish with lettuce leaves.

Baked Eggs. No. 3.

Melt a tablespoonful of butter, break the number of eggs wanted in a plate, pour butter over each. One tablespoonful of cream, pepper and salt, put in oven and bake hard or soft as desired.

Filled Eggs.

Boil hard one dozen eggs, take off the shell and cut length-wise; take out the yolks, chop up with a handful of lobster meat, a few capers, seasoning; add a little bread, fill the eggs, place in a pan and bake. Serve with cream sauce.

Fried Eggs.

One dozen eggs, two cooking spoonfuls of butter, pepper and salt. Put the butter in an iron spider and when hot drop the eggs in one by one, sprinkle over them salt and pepper; when the white is set they are soft done. Turn them over carefully with a flat cooking spoon. Drippings or lard may be used instead of butter; take the eggs up on a hot platter. They are delicious fried in ham gravy; place them around the edge of the platter and the ham in the centre.

Boiled Eggs.

Eggs should always be washed before boiling. If possible choose fresh eggs. If the skin is rough they will be likely to be fresh unless they are preserved eggs; to be nutritious, eggs should be boiled either soft or hard, cooked half way they are indigestible; it requires three minutes to cook them very soft; and four to boil them about right; cook eight or ten minutes for hard-boiled eggs; the yolk should be mealy not soggy. Always put them in boiling water and watch the clock; use an egg boiler if you have one, if not put the eggs in the water and take them out with a perforated skimmer.

Poached Eggs.

Six fresh eggs, six slices of toast, butter, pepper and salt. Use a shallow saucepan. Have the water boiling and salted; break the eggs one at a time and slip carefully into the boiling water; when all are in, place the pan over the fire until the white of each is set. Butter the toast, place an egg on each slice, sprinkle over pepper to taste.

Panned Eggs.

Make a mince meat of chopped ham, fine bread crumbs, pepper, salt and a little melted butter. Moisten to a soft paste with milk, and half fill patty pans; break an egg upon the top of each, dust with pepper and salt, and sprinkle with powdered cracker crumbs; Bake in an oven about eight minutes.

Pickled Eggs.

Boil eggs hard; after removing shell put in vinegar, pepper and salt to taste. Cut length-wise to serve.

Curried Eggs.

Boil eggs hard, then cool, mix in a saucepan two tablespoonfuls of butter and one of curry powder over a moderate fire; put in a couple of chopped onions, and fry soft, add a cup or more of broth or rich gravy and simmer until the onion is reduced to pulp. Add to this a cup of cream mixed smooth with a tablespoonful of flour, let boil up and add the eggs cut in slices; heat through and serve hot.

Snow Eggs.

Twelve eggs, one-half pound powdered sugar, one and one-half pints milk; break the eggs, separate the yolks from the whites and beat the whites stiff; add the sugar and flavor with orange or vanilla; boil the milk with a little sugar, and the flavoring, when boiling drop the whites, a spoonful at a time, and let them drip on a strainer, take half of the milk and add the beaten yolks, first diluting with a little milk; cook and turn with wooden spoon, take off the fire when the whites begin to fasten, place in a dish and pour the cream over them carefully.—An old Flemish dish

Columbus Eggs.

Take hard boiled eggs, cut in half lengthwise, take the yolks, mash fine and mix with a little of Durkees' Salad Dressing, replace in whites and serve on a small platter. Garnish with parsley or celery.

Scrambled Eggs. No. 1.

Five eggs, one ounce of butter, one tablespoonful of milk, salt and pepper to taste. Beat the eggs until light, then add the milk, pepper and salt, beat again, melt the butter in a saucepan and put in the eggs; stir them constantly with a spoon until they set. Do not cook them hard; garnish with parsley leaves.

Scrambled Eggs. No. 2.

Four eggs, one tablespoonful of butter, salt and pepper to taste; melt the butter in a saucepan, break the eggs, sprinkle in the salt and pepper, and stir constantly over a slow fire. Be very careful or they will scorch

Scrambled Eggs. No. 3.

Five eggs, half a teacupful of milk, half an ounce of butter, pepper and salt. Put the butter in a saucepan on the stove, when melted, add the milk, pepper and salt; stir together; then add the eggs without beating them. Stir one way until the whites are set.

Scrambled Eggs with Ham.

One teacupful cold boiled ham, three eggs, piece of butter the size of walnut, pepper and salt to taste and a sprig of parsley. Chop the ham fine, put the butter in a saucepan, when melted, put in the ham; allow it to simmer a few minutes. Beat the eggs and pour them over the ham, put in pepper and salt, and scramble all together, stirring slightly with a fork.

Scrambled Eggs with Tomatoes.

Fve tomatoes, tablespoonful of butter, pepper and salt to taste, four eggs, peel the tomatoes, cut them up and boil them in a saucepan with the seasoning until done, then beat the eggs and turn them in the saucepan with the tomatoes, scramble them together stirring one way for two or three minutes, then let them stand until done and serve immediately.

Light Egg Scramble.

One tablespoonful of butter, half a teacupful of bread crumbs, half a teacupful of milk, four eggs, pepper and salt. Soak the bread in the milk; beat the eggs until they are very light, then add the bread and milk, pepper and salt. Stir all together, beating one way. Melt the butter in a saucepan, pour in the mixture, stir until done. Serve hot, with buttered toast.

Omelettes.

Care should be taken in the preparation of omelettes. The whites and yolks of the eggs should always be beaten separately, the tender fluffy lightness so desirable in an omelette can only be obtained by beating the whites of the eggs to a stiff froth, and the yolks until the stringy appearance is all gone and they beat up lightly. Omelettes should never be turned, when they are done on the under side always set the frying pan on the grate in the oven to cook the top. Do not stir, shake or disturb them in any manner, only to slip a flat knife under the edge to see if the under side is browning. It is best to use lard or drippings in cooking them as butter burns easily. A little experience will soon enable one to make and take up a delicious fine looking omelette that will amply repay all the care used. Omelettes can be varied by using meat.

Oyster Omelettes.

One dozen small oysters, five eggs, one tablespoonful of milk; one tablespoonful of cracker crumbs, black pepper, salt and one tablespoonful of butter; drain the oysters, use the white part and chop it fine, soak the crumbs in the milk and add to the well beaten yolks of the eggs, put in the oysters, pepper, salt and melted butter, lastly add the whites of the eggs beaten light, and pour into a hot pan that has a tablespoonful of melted butter in it, cook as you would any omelette.

Oyster Omelette No. 2

One dozen large oysters chopped small, one half teaspoonful salt sprinkled on them, then let them stand in their own liquor half an hour; beat six eggs, yolks and whites separately, the former to a smooth paste, the latter to a stiff froth; add to the yolks a tablespoonful of rich sweet cream, pepper and salt to taste, then stir in whites. Put two tablespoonfuls of butter in a hot frying pan; when it begins to fry pour in your egg mixture, and add the oysters quickly; do not stir, but with a broad-bladed knife lift [as the eggs set] the omelette from the bottom of the pan, to prevent scorching; in five minutes it will be done. Place a hot dish, bottom upward over the omelette, and turn the pan over with the brown side uppermost upon the the dish. Serve at once.

Meat Omelette.

Five eggs, a teacupful of finely-chopped cold meat, a slice of bread, two tablespoonfuls of milk, a tablespoonful of butter, pepper and salt to taste. Soak the bread in the milk, beat the yolks of the eggs, melt the butter, stir all together, then add the meat, pepper and salt. Beat the white of the eggs to a froth, and stir in slowly. Have a frying-pan ready with butter in it heated. Pour in the mixture, and when done on the underside place in the oven for a few minutes: fold over on a hot platter and serve. Ham, veal, beef, chicken and boiled tongue are nice in this omelette.

Individual Omelette.

Prepare the same as meat omelette, and bake in large gem tins. Place the tins on the bottom of the oven until partly done, then put them on the grate. Bake slowly and do not scorch.

Bread Omelette.

One teacupful sweet milk, one teacupful fine bread crumbs without crust, salt and pepper; beat all together, add two well beaten eggs; put in a frying pan a small lump of butter, let it melt and run all over the pan; pour in the omelette, cook gently until it sets, loosen the edges and fold one half over the other; now put on a hot plate to fit the pan, hold firmly and turn the pan over, it will come out nice and whole.

Light Omelette.

Six eggs, one teacupful of bread crumbs, one teacupful of milk, one teaspoonful of butter, one tablespoonful of lard, pepper and salt to taste; beat the whites and yolks of the eggs separately, the whites to a stiff froth, the yolks thoroughly, pour the milk on the bread, mash together and add the yolks and butter, mix well together; put the lard with a pinch of salt into a frying pan and set it over the fire, mix lightly the whites with the other ingredients; and pour all the mixture into the frying pan; do not let it get too hot or it will scorch, do not stir or shake it. When the omelette sets, lift the edge carefully with a flat knife, if a light brown put the pan in the oven on the grate to cook the top; be careful not to cook it hard; as soon as the top is set it is done; take out on a platter with a griddle cake knife, folding it over as you do so, put a little butter between the folds; serve hot; this is a very light delicate omelette.

Rice Omelette.

Six eggs, three tablespoonfuls of cold boiled rice, two tablespoonfuls of milk, one tablespoonful of lard, one heaping teaspoonful of butter, pepper and salt to taste; mash the rice in the milk, add the butter, pepper and salt, and the yolks of the eggs which should be thoroughly beaten; beat the whites into a stiff froth and stir them very lightly with the mixture; put the lard and a sprinkle of salt in the frying pan over the fire, when hot pour in the omelette, do not stir it when set and a very light brown on the bottom, which you can see by lifting the edge with a flat knife, place in the oven on the grate. When the top is set it is done, garnish with lettuce and eat with buttered toast; one omelette is sufficient for four persons.

To Preserve Eggs.

To preserve eggs pack them in crocks, with coarse salt. Put salt on the bottom of the jar, and then put in a layer of eggs a little ways apart, small end down; fill between the eggs with salt, and put a layer on top of them. Continue this process until the crock is full.

To Test Eggs.

Put them in water, if the large end turns up they are not fresh; this is said to be a sure way of telling good eggs. If you are going to preserve eggs look at them through a strong light, they should be perfectly clear without a dark spot in them. A good way to tell a fresh egg is by the air bubble on the large end, fresh eggs will have a small air bubble; hold the egg up to the light or to an egg tester, turn it around slowly, if the bubble is a quarter of an inch deep at the top of the large end it should be rejected. The shell of a stale egg is very smooth, while fresh eggs have a somewhat rough shell. The contents of a fresh egg stick to the shell when cooked and must be removed with a spoon, but the shell will peel readily from a boiled stale egg like the skin from an orange; stale eggs will boil hard sooner than fresh ones; but it takes much longer to beat them to a froth than it does if they are fresh. The hand will do to test eggs sometimes, close the hand around the egg and hold it to a strong light and look through the egg; however the best way is to use an egg tester.

To Make an Egg Tester.

Take a box fasten the cover on with hinges, cut out half the front of the box in the middle, paint the inside a good black; then put one or two short candles in the middle of the opening two inches back from the front; light the candle and turn the box so that outside light will strike it but not go in the box. Now examine your eggs.

VEGETABLES.

Many housekeepers think it requires no skill to cook vegetables; this is a mistake. A table always supplied with poorly cooked vegetables indicates a very poor housekeeper.

It is just as easy to acquire a proper knowledge of cooking food so that it will be wholesome, tempting and healthful, as it is to learn to cook it poorly.

Care should always be taken in the selection of vegetables. All green vegetables should be freshly gathered; always washed in cold water, and cooked in boiled salted water till tender.

Many a good dinner has been spoiled by the potatoes having been cooked too much or too little. The cooking of potatoes is indeed an art, as they are used every day by almost all families; and one cannot be too careful about preparing them. Be careful in selecting potatoes.

Stewed Mushrooms.

Wash the mushrooms carefully in cold water, cutting off the stalks, then pare the skin. Put a tablespoonful of butter in a saucepan, add the mushrooms and a little flour; let the mushrooms cook for twenty minutes in their own liquor, then add pepper and salt; serve hot. Some add a couple of tablespoonfuls of rich cream to the sauce.

Broiled Mushrooms.

Pick out fine, large mushrooms, peel; wash carefully and cut off the ends; lay them in melted butter, sprinkle with salt and pepper; then place on an oyster, broiler; and turn when brown. Place on buttered toast, pour over melted butter. Serve hot.

Lyonnaise Potatoes, 1.

Pint of milk; tablespoonful of butter; salt, pepper; teaspoonful cornstarch; six large, cold, boiled potatoes. Put the milk in a frying pan; add butter, pepper and salt; let it boil; mix the cornstarch with a little cold milk; add, stirring until it thickens; cut the potatoes in small pieces, put all together, cook fifteen minutes, stirring to prevent burning. This is a cheap, wholesome breakfast dish.

Lyonnaise Potatoes, No. 2.

Five cold, boiled potatoes; one onion; cookingspoonful of butter; salt and pepper. Slice the onion very fine, fry in the butter until a light brown; add the potatoes, sliced, with salt and pepper to taste. Shake the sauce pan until the potatoes are hot and brown. A little chopped parsley may be added if desired.

Potato Ribbons or Strings.

Six potatoes; hot lard; salt. Peel the potatoes, cut them in quarters, pare them round and round in very long ribbons; let them stand in cold water fifteen minutes, drain in colander; fry in the hot, salted lard until they are crisp and light brown; drain, place them on a hot platter and garnish with parsley.

Potatoes Sliced.

Six large, cold, boiled potatoes, two ounces of butter; one teacupful of stock; one teaspoonful of finely chopped parsley; pepper and salt. Put the butter into a stewpan, when melted add stock or gravy, parsley, pepper and salt; stir over the fire until hot, add potatoes, simmer five minutes. Serve hot.

Potatoes Hashed and Browned.

Six large cold boiled potatoes chopped fine; put in pan with tablespoonful butter, pepper and salt to taste; let fry till a rich brown; turn out on hot platter, crisp part on top. Garnish with parsley.

French Fried Potatoes.

Five good-sized potatoes, kettle hot lard, a little salt. Peel potatoes, cut in long pieces, about half the size of the potato, cutting them lengthwise; put in cold water, drying them lightly on a towel until they are perfectly dry. Then drop into the boiling lard which has been salted. Stir them often; when they are a nice light brown, take them out with a skimmer. They will be crisp and not greasy.

Fried Potatoes.

Pare the potatoes, then slice them thin, of a uniform size, let them stand fifteen minutes in frying pan with the butter and salt, (nice beef drippings will do instead of butter.) Cover and occasionally turn them; when they are tender and of a light brown color they are done.

Duchess Potatoes.

Take six large potatoes; after they are peeled, cut in little round balls with a potato cutter, steam till tender; put some milk in skillet, about half full, little butter, pepper and salt to taste, tablespoonful chopped parsley, thicken with tablespoonful flour dissolved in water, then add the potatoes. This makes a very nice dish.

Boiled Potatoes.

Ten medium-sized potatoes, teaspoonful of salt. Pare very thin, the best part of the potato is near the skin. Let stand a little while in cold water, then put to boil in a kettle of boiling water; keep constantly boiling till done, pour off the water, partially remove the cover and stand on back of the stove a few minutes.

Boiled Potatoes with Jackets On.

Wash thoroughly several medium-sized potatoes. Pare a strip around the edge of the potato, about half an inch wide, and put on to boil in a kettle of hot water. When done, drain thoroughly, and let stand on back of stove till ready to use.

Mashed Potatoes.

Ten medium-sized potatoes, pinch of salt, tablespoonful of butter, cream or milk. Boil till done; mash fine, add butter cream or milk and salt. Stir with cooking spoon until perfectly smooth and light.

Escalloped Potatoes.

Chop fine ten medium-sized potatoes, rub inside of baking dish well with butter, then put layer of potatoes, pepper and salt, and small pieces of butter, carefully over the potatoes, then another layer, and so on, till the dish is three-quarters full; fill up with cream or milk, bake half an hour in moderately hot oven.

Stewed Potatoes.

Six large potatoes, two teacupfuls milk, teaspoonful butter, salt and pepper, teaspoonful flour. Pare the potatoes, cut them in slices, then let them lie in cold water fifteen minutes; put into a saucepan with boiling water. When nearly done pour off the water, put in the milk, salt, pepper and butter, boil; then thicken with the flour dissolved in a little cold milk; simmer a few minutes until done.

Saratoga Chips.

Pare three medium-sized potatoes, and cut in very thin slices, (with a cutter would be best) over a pan of water, so that they will drop at once into water, which makes them light and dry after being fried. Let soak a few moments; dry, few at a time on a towel and fry in hot lard. As soon as a light brown color drop on a paper in colander and sprinkle with salt, let stand in oven, continuing till all are done.

Potato Croquettes.

Two teacupfuls mashed potatoes, yolks of two eggs, tablespoonful chopped parsley, two tablespoonfuls cream, one small teaspoonful onion juice, teaspoonful salt, small piece of butter, little dash of cayenne pepper and nutmeg. Beat yolks until light. then add to the potatoes, adding the other ingredients; mix well and put in skillet; when thoroughly heated, so mixture leaves the sides of pan, remove from fire, and when cool form into croquettes. Roll in egg, dip in bread crumbs and drop in kettle of hot lard. This will make a dozen.

Potato Cakes.

Five potatoes, one egg, teaspoonful of butter, salt and pepper. Boil the potatoes and mash them while hot; beat the egg and melt the butter; stir the potatoes and add butter pepper and salt. Make into flat cakes, flour them and fry in lard or drippings until brown. Cold mashed potatoes may also be used this way. These are nice baked instead of fried.

Stuffed Potatoes.

Select medium-sized potatoes; wash clean with a brush, then bake. When done, cut each lengthwise, on one side only; take out the inside of each potato and mash all together in a pan; adding milk, butter and salt; keep hot and put back in the skins and draw together. Allow one for a person.

French Baked Potatoes.

Six large potatoes, as near the same size as possible; place in oven until half baked, then take them out and cut in halves. Make a dressing of the yolk of one egg, well beaten, and season with salt and pepper; place in oven again and leave until done. Serve on a platter, garnished with parsley.

Potatoes a la Parisienne.

Pare large, uncooked potatoes; cut little balls out of these with the vegetable scoop; drop them into ice water. When all are prepared drain them and put in the frying basket; put the basket carefully into the fat; cook ten minutes; drain, season with salt, and serve very hot. These are nice to serve with a fillet of beef; they may be arranged on the dish with the meat, or served in a separate dish.

Roast Sweet Potatoes.

Wash well potatoes of a uniform size, being careful not to cut them; let stand about a half hour in a moderately hot oven, serve immediately. These are very nice roasted on a hot hearth, or in a Dutch oven, same as common potatoes.

Boiled Sweet Potatoes.

Pick out several even-sized potatoes, wash thoroughly, being careful not to cut them. Place in kettle of boiling water; when done drain carefully and remove the corner of the lid, so the steam will all disappear. By so doing they will be mealy and dry.

Fried Sweet Potatoes.

Take four or five good-sized sweet potatoes, slice thin; have the hot lard ready; drop them in, sprinkling well with pepper and salt; brown first one side and then the other. These should be served hot.

Escalloped Sweet Potatoes.

Parboil, then peel, slice crosswise and pack in layers in a pudding dish; seasoning each layer with butter, salt pepper and a little sugar; cover thickly with bread or cracker crumbs; wet with cream; stick bits of butter in this coating, dust with salt and pepper; bake, covered, half an hour until brown.

Cauliflower.

Cut off all the green leaves of one large cauliflower, cut it close at the bottom, from the stalk; if large divide into four quarters. Let it lie in cold water for an hour, then put into boiling milk and water, or water only, milk makes it white. Skim while boiling; when the stalks are tender take it up, which must be done before it loses its crispness. Drain through a colander and serve with melted butter.

Creamed Cauliflower.

Trim and wash one head of cauliflower thoroughly, cut in pieces, boil in salted water, enough to cover; when done drain through a colander, put back in saucepan and add a half a pint of milk, small piece of butter and little pepper; thicken with one teaspoonful of flour. Cream may be used instead of milk and flour.

Buttered Parsnips.

Scrape and wash five or six parsnips and slice them lengthwise; boil in water enough to cover them until done; then drain, put in tablespoonful of butter, little salt and pepper, beat one egg, with half a teacupful of milk and turn over the parsnips.

Fried Parsnips.

Scrape and wash five or six large parsnips, boil until tender in salted water, cut in slices lengthwise, dredge in flour and fry in quarter teacupful of butter or drippings, turning when brown. The parsnips are nice dipped in egg and bread crumbs instead of flour.

Asparagus.

Cut the points of one bunch or asparagus as far as they are perfectly tender in pieces not more than half an inch in length; wash them very clean and throw them into plenty of boiling water, salted; when they are tender take out the asparagus and lay aside a few minutes. Butter five or six pieces of toast and lay on a dish, and place the asparagus on top, then pour a teacupful of milk into the saucepan, thicken with a tablespoonful of flour, little pepper and salt, and a teaspoonful of butter. Pour over the asparagus and serve hot.

Celery.

Cut off the roots, wash and scrape the stalks, rejecting the toughest; cut off the green leaves, retain the leaves that grow near the heart. If the stalks are wide, shred in two; lay in cold water until needed. Serve in long, flat celery dishes.

The habitual use of this vegetable is much more beneficial to people than many are aware of.

Celery Salad.

Two stalks celery, teacupful of cabbage, chopped; salad dressing. Lay the celery and cabbage in cold water for half an hour; cut the celery in small pieces, chop the cabbage, place in salad dish and pour the dressing over it. Mix lightly with a silver fork. Garnish with white celery leaves.

Creamed Celery.

Cut off all the roots and green leaves, lay in cold water a few minutes; cut the stalks in short lengths, and put in boiling water to cook, just as you do asparagus. When done put in a teacupful of milk, little butter and pepper and thicken with the flour.

Turnips, Mashed.

Peel five white turnips, boil; then mash fine, season with a teaspoonful of butter and a little salt. Some people mix with an equal quantity of hot, mashed potatoes.

Yellow Turnips.

These are much more solid than the white turnip and are prepared the same as the above recipe.

Summer Squash.

Cut the squash in pieces, take out the seeds and pare, unless the squash is very tender; boil or stew until soft; drain through a cheese-cloth bag, return to saucepan and season, mash all together, stir the butter in thoroughly and serve hot.

Winter Squash Boiled.

Take one-half a squash, cut in pieces, take out seeds and pare as thin as possible, boil or steam until tender in salted water; when done, drain thoroughly through a colander, return to saucepan, mash and season with butter and pepper; a good winter squash should be dry and mealy.

Winter Squash Baked.

Select a green hubbard squash, cut in pieces about five inches square, put on the grate in the oven and bake; it requires about as much time to bake as sweet potatoes and should be served immediately.

Green Corn.

Sweet corn is the best, the grain should be full, but the milk should not be hard. It should be cooked on the same day it is gathered; it loses its sweetness in a few hours, and must be artificially supplied. Strip off the husks, pick out the silk, and put in boiling water; if not entirely fresh, add a tablespoonful of sugar, but no salt. Boil quickly twenty minutes, and serve; or you may cut it from the cob, put in plenty of butter, a little salt, and serve.

Escalloped Corn.

Cover the bottom of a dish with canned corn; put in a layer of bread crumbs; pepper, salt and butter to taste; then another layer of corn, covering with bread crumbs; seasoning and butter; add milk enough to make it moist and put in oven; bake.

Green Corn Pudding.

Twelve ears of sweet corn, one quart of sweet milk, four eggs; teaspoonful of salt, tablespoonful of butter. Grate the corn and stir in the milk and salt; beat the eggs and mix all well together. Pour the mixture into a dish, put the butter on top in pieces; bake forty-five minutes in a quick oven. To be eaten hot with butter. Some add two teacupfuls of sugar.

Corn Pudding.

Grate twelve ears of tender, green, uncooked corn; add yolks and whites, (beaten separately), of four eggs;

one teaspoonful sugar, same of flour, mixed with one tablespoonful of melted butter; pepper and salt to taste. Add one pint of milk and bake about three-quarters of an hour.

Corn Oysters.

One teacupful flour, one-half teacupful melted butter, three tablespoonfuls milk, two teaspoonfuls salt, one-quarter teaspoonful pepper, one pint grated corn. Pour on the flour and beat well; then add the other ingredients and beat rapidly for three minutes. Have fat in frying pan to depth of two inches. Put in the batter by the spoonful. Fry about five minutes.

Baked Corn.

Grate eight large ears of corn, half a pint of milk, two eggs; salt and pepper to taste; one tablespoonful each of sugar and butter. Beat eggs light, add milk, grated corn, sugar, salt, and melted butter. Bake in an earthen dish until a light brown.

Green Corn Stewed.

One dozen ears of sweet corn, one teacupful of water, one tablespoonful of butter, one teacupful of milk or cream, salt and pepper to taste; cut the corn from the ears with a sharp knife; do not cut close to cob; after cutting, scrape the cob with the knife to take off the remainder of the corn without the hull; put the corn and cold water into a double saucepan or pail placed into a kettle of boiling water, and boil twenty minutes; when done, season with butter, milk or cream, pepper and salt; if the corn is not fresh, add a tablespoonful of sugar.

Green Corn Cakes.

Six ears of sweet corn, one teacupful of milk, one egg, one teaspoonful of salt, flour enough for batter, pepper to taste; grate the corn, beat the egg and stir the ingredients all together, adding flour enough to make a batter; bake on griddle as you would ordinary griddle cakes.

Green Corn Cakes No. 2.

Two teacupfuls of grated green corn, one teacupful of flour, half a teacupful of milk, half a teacupful of melted butter, one egg, teaspoonful of salt, pepper to taste; stir all together, beating well, except the egg, which should be added last, partly beaten; drop a spoonful at a time on buttered tins and bake ten or fifteen minutes, or fry, or bake on griddles.

Succotash.

One pint of sweet corn cut, from the cob, half a pint of lima beans; one teacupful of milk or cream, one tablespoonful of butter, salt and pepper. Pick all the silk from the ears, and cut the corn from the cob, cut only a little over half through the kernel, and scrape the rest from the cob with the knife; this saves the juicy sweetness without the hull. Put the corn and beans in a kettle and cover with water, adding salt. Boil until the beans are tender; when done put in the milk or cream, butter and pepper.

Ragout of Peas.

Take one quart of dry, green peas; teacupful of turnips cut very fine, same of carrots. Soak peas over night; boil in same water as soaked in; salt and pepto taste. Mix one tablespoonful of flour with same amount of butter. Cook until vegetables are tender.

Green Peas.

Put one pint of shelled peas into boiling salted water if young, boil half an hour, older ones need a longer time; when done, pour off the water, add one teacupful of milk, tablespoonful butter, pepper; set on the stove and boil slowly, dissolve one teaspoonful of flour in a little cold milk and stir in as soon as they commence to boil; cream may be used instead of milk and flour.

To Cook Canned Peas.

Drain off all the liquor from a can of peas, put into a saucepan, add a good sized piece of butter, plenty of pepper and salt; when thoroughly heated, serve; cream or milk may be added if so desired.

Ripe Peas.

One quart of peas, one tablespoonful of butter, salt and pepper to taste; soak the peas over night, then boil in salted water until done, season with butter and pepper; split ripe peas are very nice to use in pea soup also.

Puree of Peas.

Two small cans peas, one tablespoonful of butter, one bay leaf, two teacupfuls of milk, two teacupfuls water, a small onion, one tablespoonful flour or corn starch, pepper, salt, cloves, parsley to taste; wash the peas carefully in cold water, cook about a half-hour until almost dry. Press through a colander, put on the milk in a rice boiler, adding the bay leaf, onion, cloves and parsley, then rub the butter and flour or cornstarch until smooth, strain the milk, add the peas; stir in the butter and flour until it boils and thickens, lastly adding the pepper and salt; this makes an excellent soup; Lima or other beans may be made into a puree the same way.

Hygenic Baked Beans.

One quart beans, three quarts water; soak six hours, boil in same water three hours; one-half cup cream or butter; salt; then bake one hour.

String Beans.

One quart of beans, tablespoonful of butter, teacupful of milk, salt and pepper to taste. Cut off both ends of the bean, and string carefully; it spoils them to leave the strings on. Cut the beans in small pieces and let lie in cold water half an hour; drain, and put in boiling, salted water. They require considerable boiling, about an hour, at least. Cook till tender, as this is a very unwholesome vegetable when underdone. Pour off the water, add milk and pepper, then let boil a minute; serve. They are nice seasoned with butter and no milk.

Butter Beans.

One quart of beans, teacupful cream or milk, teaspoonful salt, tablespoonful butter, pepper. String carefully and wash, cut in small pieces and throw in cold water a little while. Boil in salted water, cook two hours or more, unless very tender and young. When thoroughly cooked, pour off the water, and season with cream or milk and pepper.

Lima Beans.

Quart lima beans shelled, tablespoonful of butter, salt and pepper. Look over the beans and let them lie in cold water half an hour, then put them in a saucepan of boiling water, with salt and cook until tender. Drain, and add butter and pepper. Soak ripe lima beans several hours and cook the same as green beans.

Lima Beans, No. 2.

Pint of beans, half a pint of milk, teaspoonful of butter, half a teaspoonful of flour, salt and pepper. Cook as above, drain; heat the milk to boiling; add butter, pepper and salt; dissolve the flour in a little cold milk; then stir it in the boiling milk; put in the beans and let stand a few minutes.

Boston Baked Beans.

One quart of white beans, half a pound of salt pork, one tablespoonful of New Orleans molasses, salt and pepper to taste; pick over the beans carefully, then wash thoroughly, soak over night in water enough to cover them; parboil twice, the first time put over in cold water and drain it off as soon as it begins to boil; the second time, put them in boiling water, boil only a few minutes, drain through a colander; then wash the pork and boil with the beans; some beans will soften in a few minutes, while others require an hour or more; do not allow the skin to break, but as soon as the hardness is gone, pour the beans and liquor into the bean jar, add the molasses and pepper; salt if necessary. Place the pork on top, and bake in a moderate oven ten or twelve hours. It may be necessary to add water occasionally, and be sure to keep the jar covered on top.

Carrots, Buttered.

Pare six carrots, cut in slices, (not lengthwise,) put in saucepan and pour on boiling water, with salt. When boiled, drain off the water, and put in one tablespoonful of butter; pepper to taste. Stir until the carrots are covered with the melted butter and serve hot.

Creamed Carrots.

Pare five large carrots, cut them into strips; put them into a saucepan with salt and boiling water. When done, pour off all the water, then add a teacupful of milk, a little butter and pepper. As soon as the milk begins to boil, stir in the flour dissolved in cold milk.

Beets.

Wash the beets carefully in several waters. Do not scrape or cut the skin, as it spoils the taste and color to let them bleed. Salt the water and put in the beets; boil until thoroughly cooked. Old beets take a much longer time to cook than young ones, which requires from one hour and a half to two hours. When done put in a pan of cold water and take off the skin with the hand; cut in slices. Boil the vinegar, add the butter and pepper and pour over the beets.

Beet Greens.

When the beets are small, and the leaves tender, they are very nice for greens. Wash very carefully, rejecting the wilted ones. Put in boiling salted water with half a pound of salt pork. Boil one hour, drain, cut the leaves, garnish with hard-boiled eggs cut in slices, and pickled beets sliced. The pork may be left out and the greens seasoned with butter, pepper and vinegar, after they are cooked.

Beets, Pickled.

Wash ten beets, of a uniform size, very carefully through several waters. Do not cut or scrape them. Salt the water and boil till well done. Let them lie in cold water and peel. Cut in slices, and when cool place them in glass jars and cover with vinegar.

Boiled Cabbage Creamed.

One head of cabbage, one pint of milk, two tablespoonfuls of butter, one tablespoonful of flour, salt and pepper to taste; select a young head of cabbage, or one that has small stalks; boil until tender, drain and chop slightly; boil the milk, dissolve the flour in a little cold milk, then stir into the boiling milk with the butter, salt and pepper; put in the cabbage and mix.

Fried Cabbage.

Half a head of cabbage, tablespoonful of flour, tablespoonful of butter, tablespoonful of sugar, two tablespoonfuls of vinegar, salt and pepper; slice the cabbage fine, or chop it, put into a saucepan with a little water, salt and pepper, sprinkle the flour and sugar on top and cover; stir occasionally, adding a little water as it boils dry; be careful that it does not scorch; when nearly done put in the butter and vinegar.

Boiled Cabbage.

Trim the cabbage carefully, examine the leaves, as insects or worms may be hid in them; cut the head in quarters and boil in a kettle of salted water for forty-five minutes, changing the water when partly cooked; when done, drain through a colander, chop, and add a little butter, salt, pepper and vinegar.

Tomatoes Sliced.

Select round tomatoes, remove the skin, slice nicely and serve with vinegar, sugar, pepper and salt; send to the table in chopped ice.

Tomato Salad.

Pare off the skin carefully, first lay in dish a layer of lettuce, leaves, then, the tomatoes whole, pour over this a mayonnaise dressing and serve very cold.

Baked Tomatoes.

Wash the tomatoes without breaking the skin, bake in a hot oven and serve whole, with butter, pepper and salt.

Cream Tomatoes.

Six large tomatoes, one tablespoonful butter, half a teacupful cream, pepper and salt, tablespoonful of crumbs; pare and slice the tomatoes, put in stew-pan with the salt, no water; when cooked, add cream, butter, pepper and sift in the crumbs, stirring slowly (the cream should be put in a little at a time); tomatoes should never be cooked in tin dishes as the acid eats the tin and makes the tomatoes unwholesome.

Fried Tomatoes.

Hard, ripe tomatoes, fine bread or cracker crumbs, salt, pepper and butter; cut the tomatoes in slices half an inch thick, without peeling, mix salt and pepper with the bread crumbs, dip each piece tomato in the crumbs, fry in the butter, which has been heated in a saucepan, and serve hot.

Stewed Tomatoes.

Six medium-sized tomatoes, cooking spoonful of butter, pepper and salt; peel the tomatoes, cut them in slices and stew them without water, add the salt when the tomatoes are beginning to cook, the butter and pepper just before removing from the stove; cook slowly and serve hot.

Tomatoes on Toast.

Prepare as above, and pour over nicely buttered toast.

Escalloped Tomatoes.

Butter a baking dish thoroughly, then place a layer of sliced tomatoes, small pieces of butter, pepper and salt, and a sprinkle of bread crumbs, and so on, then on top a layer of crumbs; bake covered until bubbling hot and brown quickly; a little sugar may be added to the seasoning if desired.

To Peel Tomatoes.

Put the tomatoes in a wire frying basket, pour boiling water over them, drain and peel.

Egg Plant.

Pare the egg-plant, then cut in thin slices, sprinkling each slice with salt; pile up on a dish, cover with a tin, put an iron or stone on top to press out the juice, and let stand about an hour; beat up an egg thoroughly, dip the plant first into the beaten egg then into cracker crumbs, then fry in hot lard; when brown, turn, and lay on brown paper to drain; tomato catsup is sometimes used with this dish.

Cucumbers.

Select medium-sized cucumbers of a green color, pare, cut off the hard end near the stem, and slice thin; let stand a half hour in cold, salt water; serve with chopped ice, vinegar, pepper and salt.

Fried Cucumbers.

Pare the cucumbers in thin slices, let them lie in cold water half an hour, then drain, and sprinkle with pepper and salt, dip in beaten egg and roll in cracker crumbs; have two tablespoonfuls of lard hot, throw in the slices, brown and crisp on one side, then turn carefully; when done, lay on brown paper to drain.

Dressed Spinach.

One-half peck spinach, one gill milk or cream, two tablespoonfuls butter, one hard boiled egg, one heaping teaspoonful flour, one teaspoonful salt, pepper to taste. Wash the spinach well through several waters, being careful to get all the sand out; cut the leaves into small pieces, and put into a kettle of water and salt, and boil until tender. Then strain through a colander; mix the flour and butter together and stir into the milk, which has been heated to boiling; let all boil a moment or so, then put in the spinach, mix all together, season with pepper and simmer several minutes; heap on a platter, smooth the yolk of the hard boiled egg to a flour and sprinkle on the spinach; cut the white of the egg in strips and lay over the top; garnish the edge of the platter with parsley.

Spinach.

Half a peck of spinach, one tablespoonful of butter, one hard boiled egg, one teaspoonful of salt; care should be taken in looking over spinach; sometimes it is covered with little insects; if so, reject that part as it is impossible to wash them off; pick off brown leaves, wilted ones and hard roots; wash carefully through several waters, then put into a kettle of boiling water, adding the salt, and boil a half hour; skim into a colander; when well drained return to the kettle and add butter; let stand a few minutes; before serving, cut into rather fine pieces, place in a dish and garnish with the boiled egg, sliced, to be eaten with vinegar.

Boiled Dandelions.

Pick only the young dandelions, as they are bitter and stringy after they blossom; cut the roots off, wash carefully in several waters and boil about a half hour, adding a teaspoonful of salt to the water; drain in a colander, then put into saucepan with a tablespoonful of butter, pepper, salt and vinegar, let come to a boil, then serve.

Lettuce.

Select nice, fresh heads, look over carefully, put into cold water long enough to make the leaves crisp; lay on a flat dish and cover the top with slices of hard boiled eggs; this is eaten with vinegar, pepper and salt, and sometimes sugar.

Lettuce Salad.

Prepare the lettuce the same as in the preceding recipe, and add a mayonnaise dressing—see recipe—for dressing.

Vegetable Oysters.

Wash and scrape, cut across in pieces half an inch thick, boil in salted water; when done, pour off the water, add plenty of milk or cream and season; to fry vegetable oysters, boil first, then fry in butter and season.

Kale.

Shake each head thoroughly, look over the leaves carefully, and wash in several waters; put half a pound of pork or bacon to cook in a kettle of water, with salt; when partly done, put in the kale and cook until tender; drain through a colander and cut up before serving; this is to be eaten with vinegar.

Boiled Onions.

One dozen onions, one teacupful of milk, butter, pepper and salt to taste; skin the onions and soak in cold water an hour or two, then put into a saucepan of boiling water with salt; when done, pour off the water, add milk, butter and pepper, let simmer a few minutes, thicken a little with flour, and serve.

Baked Onions.

Select medium sized onions, pick off the outer skin, and bake in a hot oven, serve whole; each person will season to taste with butter, pepper and salt; this is a nice way to cook onions,

Fried Onions.

Remove the skin, slice very thin and put on to boil, with a little salt; when tender, drain, add a tablespoonful of butter, pepper and salt, and fry; keep constantly stirring until they are brown.

SPICES, PICKLES AND CATSUPS.

Spiced Grapes.

Five pounds grapes, three pounds sugar, two teaspoonfuls cinnamon, two teaspoonfuls allspice, one-half teaspoonful cloves. Pulp the grapes; boil the skins till tender; cook the pulp and strain through a flour sieve; add it to the skins; put in the sugar, spice and one-half pint of vinegar and cook thoroughly.

Spiced Cherries.

Five pounds fruit, three pounds sugar, one pint of vinegar, one teaspoonful of cinnamon, one teaspoonful of allspice, one teaspoonful of cloves, one-half teaspoonful of mace. Stone the cherries; boil the vinegar, sugar and spices to a syrup; add the cherries and cook about two hours, till it becomes thick.

Spiced Gooseberries.

Spiced gooseberries are made same as spiced cherries.

Spiced Peaches.

One peck peaches, five pounds sugar, one pint vinegar, one ounce cinnamon, one ounce cloves. (whole spice), tied in a bag. Make a syrup of the sugar and vinegar, add fruit and spices. Lay fruit on a platter after cooking one-half hour; let the liquid cook thick, then pour over the peaches.

Spiced Currants.

Spiced currants are made precisely the same as spiced cherries.

Pickled Pears.

Eight pounds fruit, four pounds sugar, one pint vinegar. Put three cloves in each half; pare the fruit and cut in halves; make a syrup, and throw in the fruit till tender.

Pickled Crab-Apples.

Three pounds sugar, one quart vinegar, seven pounds apples. Throw in stick cinnamon, whole cloves, and mace, to taste; steam the crab-apples till they crack open, then lay them in jars; boil vinegar, spices and sugar awhile, then pour over the crab-apples.

Pickled Peaches.

Eight pounds of fruit, four pounds of sugar, one pint of vinegar; put two cloves in each peach.

Pickled Peaches No. 2.

Stir two pounds of white sugar with two quarts hot cider vinegar, boil ten minutes and skim well. Rub peaches with flannel cloth, and put cloves in each; put in jar and pour boiling hot vinegar over them; let stand a few days, then heat vinegar over again, and pour over them. Repeat this several days.

Ripe Cucumber Pickles No. 1.

Take ripe cucumbers, large and yellow, but not soft; pare and remove the seeds, cut in pieces, put in weak brine; then put in cayenne pepper, allspice, cinnamon and cloves to taste; cover with vinegar and let scald (not boil) till the cucumbers are tender. If the vinegar is *very* good, let the same in which you have scalded them, remain upon them; if not, add fresh vinegar, and one pound of sugar to six pounds of cucumbers. The vinegar may need scalding again, but not the cucumbers.

Ripe Cucumber Pickles No. 2.

Pare and cut cucumbers, boil one ounce of alum in one gallon of water; pour it over the cucumbers, and let them stand in it about three hours on the back of stove. Take out in cold water; change the water several times, to take out alum taste, and when thoroughly cold, boil until transparent in the following sweet pickle: To eight pounds fruit, take three pounds of white sugar, and one quart of white wine vinegar, and one cup of mixed spices, stick cinnamon, cassia buds, allspice and cloves, less of the last two than the others. Tie the spices in a muslin bag, and boil with sugar and vinegar; skim well, then add the fruit.

Cucumber Pickles No. 1.

One-half bushel of small cucumbers, two gills cider vinegar, one pint mustard seed, four ounces brown ginger, three ounces black pepper, three ounces allspice, one ounce cloves, one ounce celery seed, one once tumerice, beaten together in a mortar; add one-half teacupful of grated horse radish, three pounds brown sugar. Scald the vinegar; when cold add the above preparation. Put one pint salt over the cucumbers, then pour on boiling water to cover; let stand over night, turn off and add boiling water to cover again; the next day pour off and put in the vinegar.

Cucumber Pickles No. 2.

For six hundred little pickles, make a brine strong enough to bear up an egg. (cold water and salt), heat boiling hot and pour over cucumbers; let stand twenty-four hours; take out and wipe dry; scald three quarts vinegar, and pour over; let stand twenty-four hours, then pour off, and to fresh vinegar add one quart brown sugar, two large green peppers, one-quarter pound white mustard seed, two ounces of ginger root, two ounces of cinnamon, two ounces of allspice and cloves, one tablespoonful of celery seed, alum the size of a butternut; scald together and pour boiling hot on the cucumbers.

Chopped Cucumber Pickles.

Peel and chop twenty-four large cucumbers and five onions, mix one-half pint of salt to it, and let drain for several hours; when drained add black pepper, cloves and mustard seed, two tablespoonfuls of each; cover with good vinegar; add horseradish if desired; put in glass jars and cover with vinegar if needed.

Piccalilli.

One peck tomatoes, six peppers, three onions chopped not very fine; add one teacupful of salt; let this compound stand through the night; drain in the morning, add one teacupful of sugar, two teaspoonfuls ground cloves, two teaspoonfuls of cinnamon, two teaspoonfuls of white mustard seed and a little mace; put spices in a bag; add three quarts of cider vinegar; boil until soft.

Chopped Green Tomatoes.

One peck of green tomatoes, one small head of cabbage, ten onions, eight green peppers; chop very fine and add one teacupful salt; let stand a day, then drain well; add two pounds brown sugar, one ounce celery seed, one tablespoonful ground cloves, one tablespoonful ground mustard, two tablespoonfuls ground cinnamon; cover the whole with vinegar, and boil three or four hours.

Green Tomato Pickles.

One peck tomatoes, one head cabbage, eight medium sized green peppers (have two of them red), one tablespoonful cloves, one tablespoonful cinnamon, one tablespoonful allspice, two tablespoonfuls mustard seed, two pounds brown sugar, three or four onions. Slice the tomatoes the night before, and put about a teacupful of salt over them; in the morning drain them through a colander and chop quite fine, also other vegetables all together, and boil with the mustard seed in a weak vinegar for about five minutes, and drain them again. Tie the spices, part whole and part ground, just as you happen to have them, in a bag, and cook them with sugar, in about two and one-half quarts vinegar, fifteen minutes, then pour over the pickles; put in fruit cans and seal tight.

Sweet Tomato Pickles.

Fifteen pounds of green tomatoes, sliced; let stand over night with a little salt sprinkled over them; drain; five pounds brown sugar, one quart best cider vinegar, one ounce cloves, two ounces whole cinnamon; boil fifteen to twenty minutes; skim out and boil the syrup till thicker, if preferred, but it is not necessary.

Tomato Butter.

Seven pounds tomatoes, three pounds sugar; boil quite thick, then add one pint vinegar, one teaspoonful salt, one teaspoonful pepper, one teaspoonful cinnamon, one-half teaspoonful cloves. Do not strain tomatoes as for catsup.

Tomato Relish.

Twenty-four ripe tomatoes, four onions, five red peppers, four tablespoonfuls salt, nine tablespoonfuls sugar, seven cups vinegar; chop tomatoes, onions and red peppers very fine; boil all together until it gets thick.

Tomato Catsup.

One bushel tomatoes, squeeze, and sprinkle one teacupful salt over them, in the evening, and let stand until the second day, strain in thin muslin; four ounces black pepper, four ounces allspice, two ounces ginger, two ounces cloves, one ounce mace, one ounce nutmeg, one ounce cinnamon. Tie these in a bag and boil down one-half.

Gooseberry Catsup.

Nine pounds gooseberries, six pounds sugar, two pints vinegar, one teaspoonful cloves, one teaspoonful mace, two teaspoonfuls cinnamon.

Grape Catsup.

Five pounds common grapes, two and one-half pounds white sugar, one and one-half pints of vinegar, one tablespoonful each of cinnamon, cloves, pepper and allspice, one-half tablespoonful salt; boil the grapes until soft, then put through colander; put back into kettle with sugar, vinegar and spices; boil until it thickens, and bottle.

Shirley Sauce.

To six large ripe tomatoes add one green honey dew pepper, one onion, one tablespoonful salt, one tablespoonful sugar, one tablespoonful ginger and one teacupful of vinegar; chop tomatoes, onions and peppers fine, mix all together; boil one hour and bottle while hot.

BREAD, BISCUIT, ROLLS, ETC.

"Tell me where is fancy bred,"
Sang the Bard of Avon.
How is life most nourished?
Ne'er so thrives it save on
Bread that's made with Magic Yeast,
Health promoter at life's feast.

Bread-Making.

In order to make good bread, the quality of yeast must be good; you can always depend on *Magic Yeast.* The lightness or fermentation of the dough must be watched, also the heat of the oven.

In bread-making, care should be taken to always have the pan, jar or bowl in which the bread is raised, perfectly sweet and clean. The molding board, rolling pin and other utensils should also be kept clean. The best yeast and flour should be used, and pains taken in mixing and kneading. Always sift the flour once or twice, that there may be no lumps in the bread. It should be lightly kneaded towards the center of the mass, and care should be taken not to disturb it while it is rising.

While rising, bread should be kept at an even temperature, if possible do not let it get hot or cold.

Do not mix bread too stiff; it is best to have it as

soft as possible to knead it; do not put flour in when kneading for pans; enough should be put in the first time.

As bread is the main article of food in many families, much depends on its quality. If it is good and wholesome, it is healthful and nutritious; if hard or soggy, it is very injurious.

Brown bread is a very healthful article of diet, and should be used as freely as wheat bread.

Raised biscuit are a pleasant change from bread, and equally nutritious.

Hot bread and hot biscuit are considered unhealthy, but light, flaky baking powder biscuit eaten occasionally, are as healthy as any other article of diet eaten hot. For we generally eat potatoes and all other kinds of vegetables, as well as most meats just as they come from the kitchen stove.

Gems, muffins, griddle cakes and waffles also require care in the mixing; they are healthful, and a good substitute for bread, and abundantly repay all the time bestowed in acquiring the art of making them.

To make good bread is indeed an art; a careless putting together of ingredients will not do, as alas, too many young housekeepers have found to their dismay. Time, heat, patience, experience, all enter into good bread-making.

Bread No. 1.

Soak one cake *Magic Yeast* in a teacupful of lukewarm water, take three quarts sifted flour in bread pan, add one tablespoonful each, salt, sugar and lard; mix with two quarts lukewarm water, add yeast, knead thoroughly, and set in moderately warm place to rise over night; knead into loaves in morning and bake in slow oven.

Bread No. 2.

Put a cake of *Magic Yeast* to soak in a teacupful of lukewarm water; wash, pare and grate two medium sized potatoes in bread bowl, stir in one pint of boiling water, let stand a few minutes, then add flour, then the dissolved yeast; stir well; let raise; before going to bed take three pints water, all the flour you can beat in, let rise over night; in the morning take one pint of warm water, (or more) and salt enough; stir in all the flour you can, let rise, then knead, rise, or make into loaves. Don't mix all the sponge at once, but take it in quarters, (it is easier work); use flour enough to keep from sticking to kneading board. This makes six good sized loaves. Don't have to wait till afternoon to bake it, (bound to come up) *Magic Yeast* dissolves so quickly you don't have to boil and mash potatoes, and have a dozen things to wash, and besides you lose half the good of the potatoes, and boiled potatoes sour quicker than baked.

Good Bread No. 1.

Take two to three quarts flour, place in a large pan; add two tablespoonfuls of white sugar, one-half teaspoonful of fine salt, and a piece of good butter about the size of a small egg; rub well together; soak one-half cake of *Magic Yeast* in a teacupful of lukewarm water until dissolved; with this, mix a little sponge in the center of the pan of flour; let this stand an hour or more, until well raised, then mix with a pint of scalded milk, to which has been added one boiled mashed potato. The dough should not be too stiff, but free from the sides of the pan while being kneaded. After finishing, cover the dough with butter to prevent it from hardening and cracking; set in a warm place and let stand for several hours, then cut and knead into loaves, and place in pans; these should be set in a warm place; bake in moderately hot oven from three-quarters to one hour; when done, set up so as to allow the steam to escape. In no case should a cloth be thrown over hot bread, as it toughens the crust.

Good Bread No. 2.

One cake *Magic Yeast*, one quart of flour, one cooking spoonful of lard, one tablespoonful of sugar, one teaspoonful of salt, one-half pint of warm water. Soak the yeast in warm water about half an hour, then add lard, sugar and salt with the flour, then the rest of the water; knead into dough until it blisters, which will take from fifteen to twenty minutes; then put into a greased bowl; let it rise five or six hours, then make into rolls; let them rise about an hour and a half, then bake in a quick oven. If for loaves, they will require two hours for the second rising, and a more moderate oven for baking.

Bread—Mrs. C. B. Ely, Cleveland, No. 3.

Two quarts flour, one tablespoonful lard, one teaspoonful salt, one tablespoonful sugar, one pint lukewarm water, one *Magic Yeast* cake. Mix salt, sugar, the water and a little of the flour together, adding the yeast, which has been softened in one-half cup of warm water. Keep one cup of flour to use in the morning. Place the rest of the flour in the bread bowl, which should be of earthen, not tin; stir the mixture, (which consists of salt, sugar, lard, yeast; water and a little flour) into the centre of the flour a little at a time, until it is all in. Stir well, and leave the flour at the sides, to be worked in, in the morning.

Bread.

One cake *Magic Yeast*, five good sized potatoes, three pints warm water, as much flour as necessary. This will make four loaves. Set a sponge at night as follows: Boil and mash the potatoes, put them into the bread-pan, add three pints of warm water or milk, and a cake of *Magic Yeast*, softened in a little warm water, and enough sifted flour to make a rather stiff batter, and set in a warm place over night. In the morning mix as early as possible, adding flour to make a soft dough, but must not stick to the pan; knead thoroughly; then let rise twice the size it was when you stopped kneading; press the dough down in the pan, and when it again becomes light, make into four loaves, and put in baking pans. Let the loaves rise twice their original size; use a little soda if needed when mixing the bread in the morning; set the sponge at five in the evening, mix at ten, mold into loaves early in the morning.

Delicious Bread.

One cake *Magic Yeast*, six quarts flour, two coffee-cupfuls indian meal, two tablespoonfuls salt. Dissolve a cake of *Magic Yeast* in a teacupful of lukewarm water; sift flour in pan; add Indian meal, salt, and stir all together; make a hole in middle, pour in lukewarm water, add yeast and make pretty thick sponge; let it rise till light; mix in morning; it will be light if in a warm place in three hours. Mix the flour in your pan in the sponge, not so much but that it will be soft; take out, mold and knead a few minutes; put in greased pans and set in warm place to rise; when it cracks on top it is ready for the oven. You can see the cracks by holding up the pan and looking across it.

Magic Bread.

One *Magic Yeast* cake, three pints warm water or milk, flour enough to knead; soak a *Magic Yeast* cake for half an hour in a pint of warm (not hot) water, then stir in enough flour to make a batter, cover and set in a warm place to rise. When light add one quart of warm water (or scalded milk and water) and flour enough to make a batter; beat all briskly for fifteen minutes (*beat*, not stir) set again in a warm place to rise, (usually over night); when light add flour until it does not stick to the board; knead well, set in a warm place and when light mold into loaves; bake in a moderate oven, from three-quarters to one hour. Allow one pint of wetting to one loaf of bread; use more wetting if more bread is desired. In cold weather have your flour warm, and keep the sponge in a warm place when rising. A gentle, even warmth is necessary to make good bread. *Don't* let it get chilled.

French Bread.

One cake *Magic Yeast*, one quart water, teaspoonful salt, one-half teaspoonful ginger, one-half teacupful sugar, six large potatoes. Tie a small tablespoonful hops in a muslin bag, put it in a quart of cold water on the stove, let the water boil three minutes then remove the hops. Have ready the potatoes boiled and mashed fine, mix the potatoes with three teacupfuls of flour, until smooth; pour the hot water when boiling, gradually over the mixture of flour and potatoes, and stir until free from lumps; add the sugar, salt and ginger; when a little more than lukewarm add a cake of *Magic Yeast*; let stand in a warm place over night to rise; in the morning mix in a half teaspoonful soda dissolved in a tablespoonful warm water; mix, add enough flour to make a smooth dough, but do not add any more while kneading. If the dough sticks to your hands, wet them in lukewarm water; after kneading a few minutes, stretch the dough and fold it back, always kneading and folding it in the same direction, to keep the grain of the bread from breaking. Repeat this process for half an hour; cover and set in a warm place; when light sprinkle a little flour on board; take enough dough for a loaf, gather into a round loaf without molding, press the rolling pin across the center, pushing the dough on each side of pin, roll each side towards the centre, lap carefully; turn the loaf over and stretch it to give the long form, lay the loaves on flat tins that have been sprinkled with flour; when light bake half an hour in quick oven.

Brown Bread.

Two teacupfuls Indian meal, two teacupfuls sour milk, one teacupful flour, one teacupful molasses, one teaspoonful soda, and salt; steam three hours and bake ten or fifteen minutes.

Steamed Brown Bread. No. 1.

Two teacupfuls sour milk, two teacupfuls corn meal (even full), one teacupful flour, one teacupful molasses, one teaspoonful soda, one-half teaspoonful salt. Dissolve the soda in a little hot water, pour into the molasses; then add sour milk and other ingredients; steam three hours; if *very* moist on top, set in oven to dry off.

Steamed Brown Bread. No. 2.

Two teacupfuls Indian meal, three teacupfuls flour or graham meal, one-half teacupful molasses, teaspoonful of salt, one and one-half teaspoonfuls soda, one and one-half pints sour milk. Steam four hours, brown lightly in oven afterwards.

Yankee Brown Bread.

One and one-half teacupfuls rye flour, one pint of Indian meal, one pint sour milk, one teaspoonful soda, one-half teaspoonful salt, one-half teacupful molasses. Dissolve the soda in a little hot water and stir briskly into the milk until it foams. Then stir all the ingredients thoroughly together, beat the mixture hard, then put into deep, round, well buttered tins; steam two and a half hours; bake fifteen to twenty minutes.

Boston Brown Bread.

One pint rye meal, one quart corn meal, one teacupful molasses, teaspoonful of salt, one-half teaspoonful soda, cake *Magic Yeast*. Take enough warm water to make a batter as stiff as you can stir it, dissolve (soda in a little boiling water) yeast in warm water; let the bread rise till very light (usually over night), then put into deep iron pans and smooth the top with a knife. Let it rise a short time; bake six hours in a slow oven.

Corn Bread.

Two eggs, one pint sour milk, a half teacupful sugar, two teacupfuls corn meal, one teacupful flour, one teaspoonful soda, one-half teaspoonful salt, butter half the size of an egg. Dissolve the soda in sour milk, beat the eggs thoroughly, add to milk, also sugar, salt; melt the butter, add, then flour and corn meal.

Parker House Rolls.

Two quarts flour, two tablespoonfuls lard, salt; work these together at night and make a hole in the flour. In the morning make a teacupful of yeast, and let this rise about an hour; one pint scalded milk, blood-warm, two teacupfuls of sugar; put these in your pan and mix well, being careful not to stir in any flour. Set this about eight in the morning and let stand until noon, then stir all together. Then let this rise, until two hours before baking; cut into rolls and let rise; bake in hot oven.

Parker House Rolls. No. 2.

Cake *Magic Yeast*, one teaspoonful salt, one tablespoonful sugar, one cooking spoonful of lard, one pint of milk. Dissolve the yeast in teacupful warm water; Take flour sufficient to mix; scald the milk with the lard in it; prepare the flour with salt, sugar and yeast and add the milk, not too hot. Knead thoroughly when mixed at night, then roll out and cut with a large biscuit cutter. Spread a little butter on each roll and lap together. Let them rise very light, then bake in a quick oven.

French Rolls.

French rolls are made exactly the same as French bread. When light the second time form into small rolls instead of loaves; finish the same as the bread.

French Rolls. No. 2.

One pint milk, one cake *Magic Yeast*, one egg, one tablespoonful butter, one teaspoonful salt. Dissolve the yeast in teacupful warm water, add milk, and make a stiff batter; raise over night, then in morning add egg, butter and flour to make it stiff enough to knead. Let it rise, and roll out, cut with a round tin, brush with milk and fold over; put them in a pan and cover close. Set them in a warm place until they are very light; bake quickly. This makes delicious rolls.

Biscuit.

One-half cake *Magic Yeast*, one pint hot milk, one tablespoonful butter, one egg, one teaspoonful salt. Dissolve butter in the hot milk, when lukewarm stir in one quart of flour and beaten egg, salt and yeast (dissolved in a teacupful of warm water,) into dough until smooth. If winter, set in a warm place; if summer, a cool one, to rise. Work softly, and roll out one-half inch, and cut into biscuit and set to rise for thirty minutes, when they will be ready to bake.

Raised Biscuit.

Quart and one-half flour, two teacupfuls sweet milk, one-quarter pound butter, teaspoonful salt, two boiled potatoes, two eggs, one half cake *Magic Yeast*. Dissolve yeast in warm milk; sift the flour and mix the salt through it; make a hole in the center and put in the yeast and warm milk; let it stand awhile, then mash the potatoes and mix in the yeast and milk with the butter and well beaten eggs. Put it before the fire for two hours, then mix all together and let it rise until light. Use a pint of flour for shaping; cut off small pieces and shape lightly into cakes; let them rise again in the pans, and when they begin to crack open, bake in a quick oven.

Drop Biscuit.

One pint sour milk, one teaspoonful soda, one tablespoonful butter, one tablespoonful white sugar, one-half teaspoonful salt, flour enough to make batter ter thick; drop in buttered tins.

French Biscuit.

Two teacupfuls milk or water, one tablespoonful butter, one tablespoonful sugar, one teaspoonful salt; stir ingredients together and let it boil up, then remove from stove; when lukewarm add dissolved *Magic Yeast* and flour to make a stiff sponge; set in a warm place till light; then work in a very little more flour; let rise again; when light cut in rolls; crease with a knife; put a piece of butter in the middle, fold over and set in pans until very light; bake about twenty minutes.

Tea Biscuit.

One quart sifted flour, one-half teaspoonful salt, three teaspoonfuls Gillett's baking powder, small handful sugar, tablespoonful lard. Mix baking powder, sugar and salt lightly through the flour, rub lard through the dry mixture; mix with water, (it is better than milk), the colder the better, roll out soft, about one-third of an inch thick, cut with a large sized cutter, and bake in a really hot oven.

Soda Biscuit.

One quart flour, two tablespoonfuls lard or butter, two teaspoonfuls cream tartar, one teaspoonful soda, one and one-half teaspoonfuls salt, sufficient water to wet; mix lightly; bake in quick oven.

Yeast Biscuit.

Three-quarters teacupful butter or drippings, tablespoonful sugar, white of one egg, pint of warm water, one-half cake *Magic Yeast*. Make a sponge and let rise the same as bread; when ready to make into biscuit, mix the butter, sugar and egg into the dough thoroughly; form into small biscuits and put into buttered tins; let rise very light and bake in a quick oven.

Hominy Fritters.

Two teacupfuls cold boiled hominy, one small teacupful sweet milk, four tablespoonfuls flour, one egg, a little salt. Mix hominy, milk, flour, salt and the yolk of the egg together, adding the white last. Have ready a pan with hot butter and lard (half of each), drop the batter in by spoonfuls, and fry a light brown.

Hominy Croquettes.

One teacupful of cold boiled hominy, one teaspoonful melted butter, one teacupful milk, one teaspoonful white sugar, one well beaten egg. To the hominy add the melted butter and stir it well, adding by degrees the milk, till it is all made into a soft light paste; add the sugar and egg; roll it into oval balls with floured hands; dip in beaten egg, then in rolled cracker crumbs, and fry in hot lard.

Rice Fritters.

One teacupful of cold boiled rice, one pint of flour, one teaspoonful salt, two eggs, milk enough for a thick batter. Beat the eggs lightly and add, after the other ingredients are thoroughly mixed together, and bake on a griddle.

Corn Fritters.

One dozen ears of green corn, two eggs, one teaspoonful salt. Grate the corn, add the eggs and a little flour; do not beat the eggs, but stir them lightly in the corn. If the corn is old add a little milk; fry in hot butter and lard, half of each.

Crumpets.

Two teacupfuls sweet milk, one cooking spoonful butter, one tablespoonful sugar, one-half cake *Magic Yeast*, one egg, a little salt. Dissolve the yeast in a little warm water, add flour to make it the consistency of batter; scald the milk, add the butter, let cool, and add the yeast, salt, sugar and flour; beat the batter briskly ten minutes, then put in a warm place to rise, usually over night. In the morning beat the egg well and add to the batter, and put in buttered gem tins to rise. When light, bake in a moderately hot oven; serve hot. Add a little soda in the morning if necessary.

Gems.

One teaspoonful Gillett's baking powder, two teacupfuls sweet milk, one teacupful wheat flour, one teacupful graham flour, one egg, a little sugar, one-half teaspoonful salt. Beat the eggs separately and stir all well together; have ready hot, buttered gem tins; bake in hot oven.

Muffins.

Two pints milk, two eggs, one tablespoonful butter, one tablespoonful sugar, three small teaspoonfuls Gillett's baking powder, pinch salt. Make batter the stiffness of sponge cake; bake in a quick oven in hot buttered tins, or muffin rings.

Corn Muffins.

Two teacupfuls of Indian meal, two teacupfuls flour, two eggs, piece of butter size of an egg, three teaspoonfuls Gillett's baking powder, one pint milk. Sift the meal and flour, melt the butter and stir all together.

Graham Muffins.

One pint sour milk, one teaspoonful soda, one tablespoonful molasses, two teacupfuls graham flour, one teacupful wheat flour, a little salt. With baking powder use sweet milk and small piece of butter.

Indian Meal Muffins.

Two pints of Indian meal, two pints of sweet milk, one cooking spoonful butter, one cooking spoonful molasses, one teaspoonful salt, one-third cake *Magic Yeast*. Sift the meal, melt the yeast in a little warm water; stir briskly, and it will require about five hours for the batter to rise, (or over night if for breakfast). Bake in buttered rings or tins; serve hot in the folds of a napkin.

Yeast Muffins.

One and one-half pints of flour, two pints sweet milk, two tablespoonfuls butter, one-half teaspoonful salt, one cake *Magic Yeast*, three eggs. Dissolve the yeast in half a teacupful warm water, mix the milk with the flour, beat the yolks of the eggs, and with the butter melted, and salt, add to the flour; lastly the yeast. Put this to rise at nine o'clock the night before. Just before baking the next morning, beat the whites very stiff and stir slowly in the batter; put the batter into hot, greased molds; let them stand a few minutes, and bake thirty minutes in a quick oven. If these muffins should be wanted for supper, put them to rise at twelve o'clock that day.

Pop-Overs.

One teacupful milk, two eggs, one teaspoonful of butter, pinch salt. Melt butter, and use flour enough to make batter as thick as for griddle cakes.

Waffles.

One pint sour cream, one pint flour, three eggs, one-half teaspoonful soda. Thin with a little sweet milk if batter is too thick.

Waffles. No. 2.

Five teacupfuls flour, two tablespoonfuls butter or lard, one pint sweet milk, a little salt, one teaspoonful Gillett's baking powder, two eggs. Mix the milk and flour, then beat and stir in the eggs; add the melted butter or lard, and salt; beat well and add slowly the well-beaten whites of the eggs; and lastly, sift in the baking powder. Waffle batter should always be thin; if too thick, thin with milk. Bake quickly in hot greased irons; when served, sift pulverized sugar over the top.

Yeast Waffles.

Two teacupfuls flour, one-half teacupful butter, two teacupfuls milk, one-half cake *Magic Yeast*, four eggs. Beat the yolks, stir in the milk, then the flour, and butter melted, with a little salt. Dissolve yeast in two tablespoonfuls warm water, stir in, and add the well-beaten whites last. If for supper, put the batter to rise three hours before; if for breakfast, make the batter over night.

Rice Waffles.

One pint cold boiled rice, one egg, one tablespoonful butter, milk. Thin the rice with cold milk, add egg, a small piece of butter, and flour to make a batter stiff enough to bake. Use pork to grease your waffle iron.

English Buns.

One-half pound butter, two pints flour, one teacupful sugar, two teacupfuls English currants, one-half spoonful spices mixed, a little salt, one-half cake *Magic*

Yeast dissolved. Mix flour, sugar, currants, spices and salt together; soak the *Magic Yeast* in a teacupful of warm milk, add enough of the mixed ingredients to make a thin batter; cover and set in a warm place until light, then melt and add the butter, (don't make it oily) then add the remainder of the flour, and milk sufficient to make pastry dough; cover and set to rise; when light shape the dough into buns; place them apart on buttered tins; let rise again until light and bake in a quick oven from fifteen to twenty minutes.

Rusks.

Pint of warm milk, two teacupfuls white sugar two teacupfuls butter, four eggs, one cake *Magic Yeast* Soften yeast thoroughly in a little warm water; take flour enough to make a sponge; mix all together thoroughly, over night, and knead in the morning; knead down twice, and mold into form of biscuit, brush over the top with the white of an egg sweetened; let stand until light, then bake. If served for tea, the sponge should be made in the morning.

Rusks. No. 2.

Three pints of flour, one pint of sugar, one-quarter pound of butter, one-half cake *Magic Yeast*, one pint of warm milk. Dissolve yeast in the milk; rub the butter in the flour, set a sponge and put all in; mix soft. This is good for doughnuts.

Sally Lunn.

Two tablespoonfuls melted butter, one pint warm milk, three pints flour, three beaten eggs, one teaspoonful salt, one-half cake *Magic Yeast*. Dissolve yeast in half a teacupful of warm water, mix well, put in a buttered pan, cover and set to rise. When light, bake in a moderate oven.

Sally Lunn. No. 2.

Two pints flour, two pints milk, two tablespoonfuls lard, one teaspoonful salt, one tablespoonful white sugar, one cake *Magic Yeast*, three eggs. Stir the yolks of the eggs in the milk, add the flour, sugar, melted butter or lard, then the yeast dissolved in a teacupful of warm water. When risen, add a little more flour—enough to make a soft dough—then the well-beaten whites of the eggs. Bake in two pans an inch deep. If for supper, set it at one o'clock; should it rise too quickly, set it away in a cool place until time for second working, two hours before baking.

French Twists.

One quart warm water, one tablespoonful butter, one egg, one cake *Magic Yeast*, one teaspoonful salt. Dissolve yeast in coffee-cupful of warm water, add warm milk and flour enough to make a stiff batter; let it rise; when very light work in butter, egg and flour until stiff enough to roll; cut in strips, braid it, let it rise again. When light bake on buttered tins about an hour.

Rolls.

Two quarts flour, one cake *Magic Yeast*, one and one-half pints cold water, one tablespoonful lard, one tablespoonful granulated sugar, one teaspoonful salt, one teacupful warm water. Mix the flour, water, sugar and melted lard together, then add the yeast dissolved in warm water, and salt; work for twenty minutes and let rise until light; shape into rolls and let them rise again until light; bake in a well-heated oven for twenty-five or thirty minutes. It takes about two hours after the last rising, before the rolls will be ready to bake.

Johnny Cake.

Two pints sour milk, three eggs, one heaping cooking spoonful of butter, one tablespoonful sugar, one teaspoonful salt, one-half pint flour, little cornmeal, one teaspoonful soda. Beat the whites and yolks separately, put the soda into the milk, and add the sugar, beaten yolks and melted butter, stirring gently; then add enough of the flour and meal to make a rather thin batter; lastly add the beaten whites; add a little more meal if the whites make the batter too thin. Beat thoroughly. Bake in flat tins in a hot oven.

Johnny Cake No. 2.

One egg, one teacupful sweet milk, six tablespoonfuls Indian meal, three tablespoonfuls flour, three tablespoonfuls sugar, two teaspoonfuls Gillett's baking powder, a little salt. Beat the whites of the eggs separately and add last. This makes a thin batter.

Raised Breakfast Cakes.

One quart milk, one tablespoonful butter, one egg, pinch salt, one cake *Magic Yeast*. Scald milk into this while hot; put the butter next; when lukewarm add beaten egg, and yeast dissolved in a teacupful of warm water; then stir in flour enough to make a stiff batter; cover and rise over night; in the morning stir, put in muffin pans and rise again; when light bake quickly They can be made at noon, and will be ready to bake at tea-time.

Indian Meal Pancakes.

One pint Indian meal, three-quarters pint sour milk, one cooking spoonful flour, one tablespoonful butter, two eggs, a little salt, one teaspoonful soda. Dissolve soda in a very little hot water, and stir into the batter the last thing before baking, add other ingredients, beating the eggs well. Bake on a buttered griddle; serve hot.

Oat Meal Batter Cakes.

Two teacupfuls cooked oat meal, one teacupful flour, two teacupfuls sweet milk, two teaspoonfuls Gillett's baking powder, two eggs, salt to taste. Mix the oat meal and flour in the milk, until thoroughly mixed, then add the thoroughly beaten yolks and salt. Beat the whites to a froth, and stir in gradually; add the baking powder. Fry on a hot greased griddle.

Sour Milk Pancakes.

One pint sour or buttermilk, one egg, a little salt, small teaspoonful of soda; add enough flour to make a rather stiff batter; beat thoroughly, bake on hot griddles.

Buckwheat Cakes.

One teacupful flour, two teacupfuls buckwheat flour, one tablespoonful salt, one cake *Magic Yeast*. Dissolve yeast in a cup of warm water, mix with enough water to make a stiff batter, and set to rise over night. In the morning add sufficient water to make the batter run when poured on the griddle. They are nice with a little Indian meal instead of flour.

Bread Crumb Pancakes.

One pint bread crumbs, one-half pint flour, a little salt, one egg, milk for a thin batter, two teaspoonfuls Gillett's baking powder. Crumb the bread very fine and pour upon it enough milk to cover, let soak several hours (or over night). When ready to use, beat the bread crumbs smooth, add the egg well-beaten, flour, salt, and enough milk to make a thin batter. If the milk is sour, add half a teaspoonful of soda to the milk and leave out the baking powder.

Griddle Cakes.

One pint of milk, one teaspoonful salt, two teaspoonfuls Gillett's baking powder, one egg. Stir all together, add sufficient flour to make a thick batter and fry them on the griddle.

Green Corn Cakes.

Green corn grated, one teacupful flour, one-half teacupful milk, one-half teacupful melted butter, one egg, one teaspoonful salt, a little pepper. Mix a pint of grated green corn with the flour, melted butter, salt and pepper. Drop on a buttered pan by the spoonful and bake or fry for ten or fifteen minutes.

Flannel Cakes.

Two ounces of butter, one pint of hot milk, one pint of cold milk, four beaten eggs, one teaspoonful salt, one-half cake *Magic Yeast*, flour. Put the butter into the hot milk, let it melt, add then the cold milk, the eggs, salt, the yeast dissolved in two tablespoonfuls warm water, and sufficient flour to make a stiff batter. Set it in a warm place to rise for three hours, then fry on the griddle.

Rice Cakes.

Two teacupfuls sweet milk, two teacupfuls flour, one-half teacupful boiled rice, one teaspoonful butter, one teaspoonful Gillett's baking powder, one egg, a little salt. Beat the yolks of the eggs very light, add the milk, flour, rice, lard or butter melted, and the salt. Beat all well together, then stir in the whites beaten to a froth, then sift in the baking powder. Bake on a hot greased griddle. The rice must be soft enough to mash with a spoon.

Rye Gems.

One egg, one-half teacupful sugar, one teacupful buttermilk, one teaspoonful Dwight's Cow Brand Soda, one teacupful rye meal, two-thirds teacupful flour, two tablespoonfuls melted butter. Mix in the order given, and bake in hot gem pans.

Rye Breakfast Cakes.

Two teacupfuls of rye meal, one-half teacupful molasses, a little salt, one and one-half cups of sour milk to mix it very soft, one teaspoonful of Dwight's Cow Brand Soda. Bake at once in a roll pan or muffin rings.

Muffins.

Three teacupfuls of flour, two teaspoonfuls of cream of tartar, one teaspoonful of Dwight's Cow Brand Soda. Mix it with one egg, one tablespoonful of sugar, three of melted butter, a little salt, and two teacupfuls of sweet milk. Bake in gem pans.

Muffins No. 2.

One quart flour, two teacupfuls milk, one-half teacupful sugar, two eggs, two teaspoonfuls pure cream tartar, one teaspoonful Dwight's Cow Brand Soda, a little salt, butter the size of an egg. Melt the butter with four tablespoonfuls of boiling water. Beat thoroughly. Bake in muffin pans thirty minutes in a quick oven.

Rye Muffins.

Two teacupfuls sour milk, three teacupfuls rye meal, one teacupful flour, one small teacupful molasses, two eggs, one teaspoonful Dwight's Cow Brand Soda, a little salt.

Corn Meal Muffins.

One pint of sour milk, one teaspoonful Dwight's Cow Brand Soda, one egg, one teaspoonful of salt, stiffen with corn meal, adding a small quantity of flour.

Graham Muffins.

Two teacupfuls Graham flour, one teacupful flour, two tablespoonfuls molasses or one tablespoonful sugar, one teaspoonful Dwight's Cow Brand Soda, two teaspoonfuls pure cream tartar, salt. Mix with milk, or use one egg and mix with water.

Spoon Corn Bread.

Scald one pint of meal; when cold, add one teacupful of milk, three well-beaten eggs, pinch of salt, and one small teaspoonful of Dwight's Cow Brand Soda and one of pure cream tartar. Bake one hour in a pudding dish.

Waffles.

One quart sour milk, three eggs, a small teacupful of butter or lard, two teaspoonfuls of Dwight's Cow Brand Soda dissolved in warm water, salt and flour enough to make a thick batter. Beat eggs separately until very light.

Breakfast Gems.

One teacupful sour milk, one teaspoonful salt, one teacupful rye or Graham flour, one-half teacupful of white flour sifted with one even teaspoonful of Dwight's Cow Brand Soda, one-fourth teacupful molasses. Before beginning to make the gems, place the gem pans in the oven to get very hot; then mix the milk, molasses and salt together, add the flour, stir the whole thoroughly, and bake one-half hour.

P. S.—Dwight's Cow Brand of Soda being pure, care should be exercised; do not exceed the quantities of soda named in the recipes.

MACARONI AND CHEESE.

Baked Macaroni.

One-half pound grated cheese, one-half pound macaroni, one teacupful sweet cream, two ounces of butter, salt and pepper. Break the macaroni in small pieces, put in a sauce pan with plenty of water and add one teaspoonful salt, and boil rapidly till tender, being careful not to let it stick. Then throw in cold water a moment, drain, and line a baking dish with butter, then a layer of macaroni, a layer of grated cheese, then salt and pepper sprinkled over, then another of macaroni, and so on till the macaroni is used up; put bits of butter over the top, add cream and bake in a quick oven. Serve in a baking dish.

Oysters and Macaroni,

Boil the macaroni till tender, cut in small pieces, put enough melted butter in a baking dish to just cover the bottom, then put in a layer of macaroni, then a layer of fresh raw oysters, sprinkle with salt and bits of butter, then another layer of macaroni, alternating with layers of oysters till you have the desired quantity, finishing with macaroni. Sprinkle the top with grated cheese and bits of butter. Bake until brown.

Macaroni with Cream Sauce.

Boil one-half pound of spighetti in salted water, the same as in the preceding recipe, drain and put into a heated dish and pour over it cream sauce. See SAUCES, for cream sauce.

Macaroni with Tomato Sauce.

Put one-half pound of macaroni in a pan in salted water to boil, but first break in small pieces; let boil about twenty minutes, drain, and put in a hot dish, pour Tomato sauce over it and serve immediately.

Fondue.

Put into a small saucepan one tablespoonful butter, one tablespoonful flour; stir over the fire until they bubble, then add one gill of milk or cream, stir well to prevent burning; when smooth, stir into it three ounces of finely-grated cheese of a fine quality, a scant saltspoonful of salt and a tiny pinch of cayenne; turn it into a bowl and stir into it the beaten yolks of two eggs; thoroughly whisk the whites of three eggs solid; stir them in very gently the last thing. Butter a silver chafing dish and pour the fondue into it. Bake a golden brown in a quick oven. Must be served the moment it leaves the oven or it will fall.

Cheese Fondue.

One cup fine bread crumbs, two cups fresh milk, one-half pound old cheese grated, three eggs whipped, one teaspoonful of melted butter, pepper and salt, one-half teaspoonful Gillett's Cream Tartar baking powder. Mix the eggs and milk together, and grate first the cheese, then the bread crumbs on top. Put in a dish and bake in a quick oven until delicately brown.

Cheese Straws.

Mix four tablespoonfuls flour with one large teaspoonful butter, add four tablespoonfuls of grated cheese; mix well, as you would for pie crust; season with one-half teaspoonful salt and pinch of pepper; mix all together and wet with one egg, and roll out very thin, about like pie crust; sprinkle grated cheese over and roll, and cut in long, narrow strips. Bake in moderate oven a light brown.

Cheese Toast.

Toast nice thin slices of bread crispy and brown; put on a warmed plate, allowing a piece to a person, and pour over it melted cheese. Serve while warm, and a little prepared mustard may be put on the toast before adding the cheese if so desired. New cheese is the best to melt.

Cheese Scollop.

Three eggs, one teacupful grated cheese, one teacupful bread crumbs soaked in one pint of sweet milk; beat the whites and yolks separately; little butter and salt. Bake one-half hour.

Cheese Ramakins.

Put two ounces of bread without crust and one gill of milk on to boil, stir and boil until smooth, then add four tablespoonfuls of grated cheese and two ounces or two even tablespoonfuls of butter; stir this over the fire one minute; take off, add the yolks of two eggs, salt and cayenne pepper to taste; beat the whites of three eggs to the stiffest froth; stir them carefully into the mixture; turn into a greased baking dish and bake fifteen minutes in a quick oven.

Schmier Kase.

Some call it cottage cheese. It is made from clabbered milk. Take the cream off the top of a pan of thick sour milk, let it stand in a warm place on the back part of the range, and pour over it a couple of quarts of boiling water; pour into a bag and let it drain, and hang up over night. When ready to use it, mix some rich cream, salt and pepper, and serve in ball shape.

Welsh Rarebit.

One-fourth pound rich cream cheese, one-fourth teacupful cream or milk, one teaspoonful mustard, one-half teaspoonful salt, a few grains of cayenne, one egg, one teaspoonful butter, four slices toast. Break the cheese in small pieces, put into milk in farina boiler, toast the bread and keep it hot. Mix mustard, salt and pepper, add eggs, and beat well; when cheese is melted, stir in the egg and butter, and cook two minutes, or until it thickens a little, but do not let it curdle; pour over the toast. Many use ale instead of cream.

Welsh Rarebit. No. 2.

Toast four slices of bread, spread with mustard moistened with a little hot water. Melt in a pan one-half pound cheese, with a little piece of butter. When melted, pour over the bread.

Fried Cream.

One pint of milk, good half teacupful sugar, butter the size of a hickorynut, yolks of three eggs, two tablespoonfuls cornstarch, one tablespoonful flour, stick of cinnamon one inch long, one-half teaspoonful Gillett's Double Extract of Vanilla. Put the cinnamon into the milk, and when it is just about to boil stir in the sugar and the cornstarch and flour, the two latter rubbed smooth with a little cold milk. Stir it over the fire for fully two minutes to cook well with the starch and flour. Then take off the stove and stir in the beaten yolks of the eggs, and return it a few moments to set them. Now, again taking it from the fire, remove the cinnamon, stir in the butter and vanilla, and pour it into an oblong buttered tin an inch high. When cold and stiff, cut the pudding into parallelograms, about three inches long and two wide, roll in cracker crumbs, stir in eggs (slightly beaten and sweetened), then again in the crumbs, dip in hot lard; when nice color take out, place in oven five minutes to soften the pudding; sprinkle sugar on top.

PASTRY AND PIES.

Rules to be Observed in Making Pies.

Do not use flavors or spices in fruit pies; they spoil the flavor.

Never make pies of juicy fruits without flouring the fruit.

Custard, cocoanut, cranberry, cream, lemon, meringue and apple meringue, require only one crust.

Always wet the edges of the under crust of two crust pies with water, or flour and water, before putting on the upper crust; it will make them adhere together and prevent the juice from boiling out. Always cut a slit or figure in the upper crust to allow the steam to escape.

Prepare the fruit for the pies, then gather together everything necessary ready for use; wipe the molding board and rolling-pin; grease either tins or plates (plates are nicest); have the sugar and spice-box handy. Then make the piecrust and roll it out immediately. The oven should be a hot, even temperature, and should be ready before you make your pies. Do not cool your pies quickly; they should be allowed to stand where they will cool gradually. Fruit pies are nicest made the same day they are to be used. It always shows a nicety of housekeeping to sift a little sugar over the top of pies when they are taken from the oven. Do not allow pies to stand on pie-tins; it spoils the under crust.

Use three-fourths as much butter by weight as you do flour; mix in lightly with as little water as possible. If you do not mix the butter in thoroughly the paste will be flaky and rich. Good for patties.

Pie Crust No. 1.

Four teacupfuls of flour, one teacupful and a half of lard, half a teacupful of water, half a teaspoonful of salt; sift the flour, mix in the salt and rub in the lard until it will form a ball when held tightly in the hand; then mix with the water. The lard should be cold and hard, and use cold, not ice-water. Do not mold or knead the dough, but squeeze it lightly together; cut off enough for one crust at a time and roll out gently. Many prefer butter to lard. It will require two teacupfuls of butter to four of flour. This is preferable to puff paste for nearly every kind of pastry.

Pie Crust No. 2.

Sift the flour, add a little salt, use a third as much lard as flour, by measure; rub the flour in the lard and mix with as little cold water as possible. Squeeze the dough together (do not mold or knead it), cut off enough for one crust at a time and roll out lightly; have the lard cold and hard, and use cold, not ice water. This crust is better than the crust with the lard rolled in.

Custard Pie.

One pint of milk, three eggs, half a teacupful of white sugar, half a teaspoonful of Gillett's Double Extract of Vanilla. Line your pieplate with paste. Beat the eggs well, add sugar, etc., and pour on the crust and bake immediately in a moderate oven. Do not allow it to boil or it will be spoiled, as it will curdle or whey. It should be slightly tinted when done.

Custard Pie No. 2.

Three eggs, three tablespoonfuls of sugar and milk enough to fill the pieplate; beat the yolks of the eggs thoroughly, add the sugar and milk and stir together, then add the whites of the eggs beaten to a froth, mix well together, and put in a deep pieplate lined with a rich pie paste, sprinkle a little cinnamon over the top, and bake in a moderate oven. The custard must not boil. This pie is nice flavored with Gillett's Double Extract of Vanilla.

Rhubarb or Pie Plant Pie.

Wash the rhubarb, peel off the skin and cut in small pieces, the smaller the better, line pieplates or tins with crust, sprinkle flour over the rhubarb and lay it in the crust, cover thickly with sugar and sprinkle with flour; then roll out the upper crust, cut one long and several small gashes in it, wet the edge of the under crust and cover the pie with upper; press the edges together, mark with a fork and bake in a moderate oven.

Raspberry Pie.

Look over the berries carefully, do not wash them; line a deep pie tin or plate with crust, fill with the berries, sift over a little flour and cover with sugar, wet the edge of the crust with cold water, roll out and gash the upper crust and lay it over the berries, pinch the edges gently together, taking care that they adhere firmly, and bake in a moderately hot oven.

Blackberry Pie.

Look over the berries carefully and have them ready before the crust is rolled out. Dust them with flour before putting them in the pie, roll out the crust, put a little sugar in the bottom of the crust before putting in the berries, then cover with sugar.

Blackberry Pie No. 2.

Look over the berries carefully and dust them with two tablespoonfuls of flour for each pie, roll out the crust and line a deep pie tin or plate, put in a little sugar before you do the berries, heap the berries toward the middle and cover with sugar, use a teacupful of sugar for each pie, wet the edge of the under crust before putting on the upper, break off the crust carefully with the fingers instead of cutting with a knife, and pinch the two carefully together, being sure they adhere, mark with a fork, cut gashes in the upper crust before putting it on the pie.

Apple Pie.

For pies use only sour, juicy apples; peel and cut them in thin slices, grease the tins, roll out the under crust and lay in the sliced apples. If the apples are very sour put in enough granulated sugar to cover them; if medium apples, less sugar will do; (for fine flavored apples do not use cinnamon, nutmeg or butter.) The most delicious pies are made of the pure fruit and sugar. Wet the edge of the lower crust before putting on the upper crust, pinch both carefully together until they adhere, then with a fork mark the edges.

Strawberry Pie.

Pick over and wash the berries, if they are sandy, and drain through a colander, roll out a crust and put it in a buttered pie tin, put in the berries, cover with sugar, sift over about a tablespoonful of flour and cover with the top crust which has been perforated with holes or cut in a fancy figure. Be very careful about the crusts adhering together; wet the under crust with cold water before putting on the upper; mark with a fork. Butter may be added, but will spoil the flavor.

Mince Pie.

Three pounds of cold boiled lean beef, twice the amount of sour apples, three pounds of raisins, two pounds of English currants, half a pound of suet, half a pound of citron, two tablespoonfuls of butter, two pounds of sugar, one pint of cider vinegar, one pint of New Orleans molasses, a teaspoonful each of ground cloves, cinnamon, mace, and black pepper, one nutmeg, two tablespoonfuls salt. Mince the meat fine, chop the apples, stone and partially chop the raisins, carefully wash and dry the currants, cut the citron in fine pieces, chop the suet and melt the butter. Use twice as many chopped apples by measure as you do meat. Mix all together thoroughly, put it in a porcelain kettle and scald. If the mince meat is too dry, add a little warm water when you use it. More seasoning can be used if preferred. Make a rich paste and bake with two crusts in pie tins. These pies will keep several days in winter; take them off the tins and freeze them or keep them in a cool place. Can this mince meat, or, in the winter, cover in a crock and put it in a cold place to freeze.

Washington Pie.

Two eggs and one teacupful of sugar well beaten together, a pinch of salt, four tablespoonfuls of cold water, three teaspoonfuls of Gillett's Baking Powder sifted into a teacupful of flour; bake, and when cold, split and spread with a cream made of one egg, one-half teacupful of ginger, one teacupful of sweet milk and one teaspoonful of corn starch; flavor with Gilletts' Double Extract of Vanilla or Lemon to suit the taste.

Lemon Pie.

Two eggs, one teacupful of sugar, one lemon, two heaping tablespoonfuls of flour, one teacupful of water. Wash the lemon, grate the yellow part of the peel (the white is bitter, do not use it), and squeeze out all the juice. A lemon squeezer is the best thing to squeeze lemons with. Beat the yolks of the eggs, add the sugar, lemon and flour which has been dissolved in a little of the water. Stir all together to a cream and add the water gradually; use a pinch of salt. Line a deep pieplate with nice, rich crust, pinch the edge into a high cup shape so that it will stand up above the plate, pour in the custard and bake in a moderately hot oven; when done, cover with a frosting made of the whites of the eggs and two tablespoonfuls of pulverized sugar; put the pie in the oven a few minutes to cook the frosting; it should be slightly tinted.

Lemon Pie. No. 2.

Line a deep pan with a rich paste, and for filling use the juice and rind of one lemon, four eggs (leave out the whites of three), one teacupful sugar, three-fourths teacupful of cold water, one tablespoonful flour, butter half the size of an egg. Dissolve the flour in the water, then stir in the sugar, beaten eggs, etc. After the mixture is in the crust, cut up the butter in little bits and put it around the pie. After all is baked, beat up the whites with a little sugar, spread on top and brown a little.

Lemon Mince Pie.

One lemon, one egg, one teacupful of sugar, one teacupful of raisins, one teacupful of cold water, two teacupfuls of flour, one teaspoonful of butter, a pinch of salt. Wash the lemon, grate off the yellow part of the rind and squeeze out the juice, mix with the sugar, flour and water, stone and chop the raisins, melt the butter, beat the egg thoroughly and stir all the ingredients together. Bake with two crusts. When done, sift powdered sugar over the pie while it is warm. This is an old, well-tried recipe, and a very nice pie.

Cherry Pie.

Have the paste ready, the cherries pitted and everything handy; then roll out the under crust and spread it on a greased pie tin or plate (a deep earthen pie plate is best); sprinkle a little flour and sugar over the crust, dust two tablespoonfuls of flour over the cherries and put them in the crust, cover them with white sugar and wet the edges of the crust with flour and water. Roll out the upper crust, cut one long and several short gashes in it and put it on the pie, pinch the crusts carefully together, mark the edges with a fork and bake in a moderately hot oven.

Gooseberry Pie.

This pie is made after the recipe for cherry pie, adding a little more sugar.

Currant Pie.

Made the same as cherry pie, adding more sugar if necessary.

Peach Pie.

Line the pie tin with rich pastry, slice the peaches, fill the crust, rounding the fruit toward the middle, cover with sugar, sprinkle with flour; cover with an upper crust and bake. Sprinkle pulverized sugar on top of the pie when done.

Cranberry Pie.

Roll out a nice, rich paste, and line the pieplate; fill with cold cranberry sauce, lay strips of paste across the top and bake.

Mock Mince Pie.

One teacupful molasses, one teacupful sugar, one-half teacupful vinegar, one-half teacupful butter. Boil for a few minutes, add three crackers, two eggs well beaten, one-half pint of chopped raisins, spice to taste, one tablespoonful mixed spice. Line a pie tin with nice, rich paste, and have the upper crust very flaky, make a few slits in the center for air and bake.

Cream Pie.

Line the bottom of a deep tin or plate with rich paste, bringing it well up on the sides, so it can be creased. Three eggs beaten separately; take yolks and beat in one large teacupful of sugar, one heaping tablespoonful flour, beat all together, add one pint cream, one-half pint milk, then the beaten whites. Take out before it gets thick in the middle; grate a little nutmeg on top after it is done.

Pumpkin Pie.

One pint of stewed pumpkin strained through a vegetable strainer, four eggs, one coffeecupful of sugar, a teaspoonful of ginger, a little allspice and a pinch of salt. Beat the whites and yolks of the eggs separately, mix the yolks thoroughly with the other ingredients and add enough milk to fill two deep pie plates; lastly add the whites of the eggs and stir lightly. Roll out the crust, cut it a little larger than required, lay it in the plate and pinch the edges all around, so that they will stand up cup shape, then put in the filling and bake without upper crust. Have a moderately hot oven, but do not allow the pie to boil.

Squash Pie.

Make the same as pumpkin pie, only use cinnamon instead of allspice.

Cocoanut Pie.

Three eggs, one teacupful of grated cocoanut, one teacupful of sugar, one and one-half teacupfuls milk, one tablespoonful of butter, one teaspoonful Gillett's Double Extract of Lemon, a little salt. Line a deep pie tin or plate with rich crust, form the edge into a cup shape, so that it will hold the custard. If dessicated cocoanut is used, it should be soaked in milk several hours. Beat the yolks to a froth and add sugar, milk, etc.; lastly add the whites of the eggs beaten to a foam, stir in lightly and put into the crust. Bake in the oven until the filling is done. The crust should be a very light brown.

PUDDINGS.

Kiss Pudding.

Boil one quart milk, stir into it four tablespoonfuls cornstarch dissolved in a little milk, four tablespoonfuls sugar and yolks of four eggs. Beat the whites of the eggs and add teacupful pulverized sugar, spread on top and brown lightly. Serve with cream.

Indian Pudding No. 1.

Boil one quart milk; while boiling stir in a small teacupful cornmeal and one teaspoonful salt; when cool, beat three eggs, sugar to taste, also spices, ginger and cinnamon, one-half teacupful raisins, a little bit of butter on top; stir these in pudding dish, then add one pint cold milk; bake two hours.

Indian Pudding No. 2.

One teacupful cornmeal, one teacupful molasses, one egg, one quart milk. Boil the milk, mix the other ingredients together, add the milk and season with spices. Bake one hour.

Baked Indian Pudding.

Two quarts scalded milk with salt, one and one-half teacupfuls Indian meal (yellow), one tablespoonful ginger, letting this stand twenty minutes; one teacupful molasses, two eggs (saleratus if no eggs), a piece of butter the size of a common walnut. Bake two hours. Splendid.

Boiled Indian Pudding.

Warm a pint of molasses and one of milk, stir well together, beat four eggs and stir gradually into molasses and milk; add a pound of suet chopped fine, Indian meal to make a thick batter, a teaspoonful cinnamon, nutmeg and a little grated lemon peel, and stir all together thoroughly; dip cloth into boiling water, shake, flour a little, turn in the mixture, tie up, leaving room for the pudding to swell, boil three hours. Serve hot with sauce.

Spanish Pudding.

Put two ounces of butter and a little salt in a pint of water, and when it comes to a boil add as much flour as will make it to the consistency of hasty pudding. Keep it stirred. After it has been taken from the fire and has become cold, beat it up with three eggs, and a little grated lemon peel and nutmeg. Drop the batter with a spoon into the frying pan with boiling lard and fry quickly. Sprinkle with sugar before sending to the table.

Fig Pudding No. 1.

One teacupful suet chopped fine, two eggs, one teacupful sugar, two teacupfuls bread crumbs, one-half pound figs, salt to taste. Chop figs, add suet chopped separately, then milk, eggs and sugar.

SAUCE.—One teacupful sugar, one-third teacupful butter, one egg, one-half teacupful port wine (or sherry), one teacupful milk. Mix the sugar and butter to a cream, add the egg, heat the wine and milk separately and add to the sugar.

Fig Pudding No. 2.

One pound figs chopped fine, one teacupful bread crumbs, one teacupful flour, one teacupful chopped suet, one teacupful molasses mixed with tablespoonful soda, one teacupful sour milk, three well-beaten eggs, one teaspoonful salt; steam two and one-half hours. Serve with sauce.

SAUCE.—One teacupful brown sugar, one tablespoonful cornstarch, one-half teacupful butter, yolks of two eggs; stir to a cream. Beat the whites to a stiff froth, add the other ingredients, place over a tea-kettle and add one-half teacupful of boiling water; stir well while boiling. Flavor with brandy or Gillett's Double Extract Lemon.

Strawberry Pudding.

One egg, two teacupfuls flour, one teacupful milk, one-half teacupful sugar, one-half teacupful butter (melted), one-half teaspoonful soda, one teaspoonful cream tartar, one pint crushed strawberries. Steam two hours.

SAUCE.—Two scant teacupfuls sugar, white of one egg beaten stiff, three-fourths teacupful butter beaten to a cream, one teacupful crushed strawberries; put on ice.

Suet Pudding No. 1.

One teacupful suet chopped fine, one teacupful molasses, one teacupful sweet milk, three and one-half teacupfuls flour, one teacupful fruit, one teaspoonful soda, one teaspoonful each of cinnamon, cloves and allspice. Steam two hours.

SAUCE.—One teacupful sugar, one-half teacupful butter beaten to a cream, one and one-half teacupfuls boiling water, two tablespoonfuls cornstarch (not heaping) dissolved in cold water, then stir into boiling water to cook. Take off stove, stir in butter and sugar and beat with an egg-beater. Flavor to taste.

Suet Pudding No. 2.

One-half teacupful suet chopped fine, one-half teacupful New Orleans molasses, one-half teacupful sour milk, one teacupful chopped raisins, one-half teacupful Santa currants, one-half teaspoonful cloves, one teaspoonful cinnamon, one-half teaspoonful nutmeg, one-half teaspoonful soda, flour to make thick; steam three hours. Serve with sauce.

Suet Pudding No. 3.

One teacupful molasses, one teacupful suet chopped fine, one teacupful milk, one teacupful seeded raisins, three and one-half teacupfuls flour, one teaspoonful of each of the spices, one tablespoonful soda dissolved in the molasses. Steam three hours and eat with sauce.

Black Pudding.

One teacupful black molasses, one-fourth teacupful butter, one-half teacupful of sour milk, two teacupfuls flour, one-half teaspoonful soda, one-half teaspoonful cinnamon, and allspice. Steam one hour, then set in oven five minutes.

Sauce.—One teacupful sugar, three-fourths teacupful of butter mixed to a cream, one egg, one tablespoonful vinegar. Cook in rice boiler.

Steamed Apple Pudding.

One teacupful chopped apples, two teacupfuls flour, one teaspoonful soda, one-half teacupful molasses, one teacupful sweet milk. Steam two hours.

Sauce.—One-half teacupful milk, one egg, one teacupful sugar. Let the milk scald, add the egg and sugar, which has been beaten together with an egg-beater; flavor with Gillett's vanilla.

Apple Sago.

Make just the same as apple tapioca, using sago instead of the tapioca.

Apple Pudding.

Two teacupfuls of stewed apples, one teacupful of butter, one teacupful of sugar or more if the apples are very sour, two lemons and six eggs. While the apples are hot, stir in the butter, sugar, lemon juice and the yellow part of the lemon peel grated. When cold, add the well beaten yolks of the eggs. Put a thin pie crust in the pudding dish and pour the above mixture on it and bake half an hour. Make a frosting of the whites of the eggs and a teacupful of pulverized sugar; when the pudding is done, put the frosting on it and return it to the oven for a few minutes. It should be tinted a light brown.

Apple Batter Pudding.

One pint of rich milk, two teacupfuls of flour, four eggs, one teaspoonful of salt, half teaspoonful of soda dissolved in hot water; peel and core eight apples carefully, cut them up, spread over the bottom of dish. Bake one hour and serve hot with sweet sauce.

Apple Meringue Pudding.

One pint stewed apples, three eggs, half teacupful of white sugar, one teaspoonful of butter, one teaspoonful nutmeg and cinnamon mixed; sweeten and spice, and while the apple is still very hot, stir in the butter and, a little at a time, the yolks; beat all light, pour into a buttered dish and bake ten minutes; cover without taking from the oven with a meringue made of the beaten whites, two tablespoonfuls sugar and Gillett's double extract of almond. Brown very slightly; eat cold with cream.

Corn Starch Pudding.

One pint of milk put in a farina boiler, add the yolks of two eggs well beaten, two tablespoonfuls of sugar and one and a half tablespoonfuls of corn starch dissolved in a little cold milk, and a pinch of salt; let it boil till it thickens, then flavor with Gillett's vanilla. Pour into a pudding dish, beat the whites of the eggs with a little sugar, pour on the pudding and place in the oven to brown.

Chocolate Pudding No. 1.

One pint of milk, one and a half tablespoonfuls of corn starch, half teacupful of sugar, one ounce of grated chocolate; boil the milk, stir in corn starch and sugar, lastly add the chocolate and a little Gillett's extract vanilla. Some use this with a frosting on top.

Chocolate Pudding No. 2.

One quart milk, one teacupful of sugar, three or four heaping tablespoonfuls corn starch; mix corn starch and sugar, boil milk, add two tablespoonfuls chocolate; flavor with Gillett's double extract of vanilla.

Cherry Pudding.

One pint of milk, one egg, three teacupfuls of flour, two teaspoonfuls of Gillett's cream tartar baking powder, one tablespoonful melted butter, half teacupful of sugar, half pint of stoned cherries. Steam an hour and a half.

Iced Cherry Pudding with whipped Cream.

For the medium sized molds of iced cherry pudding use a quart of Morella cherries, which are very juicy and sour, meantime put a pound of granulated sugar over the fire with a gill of cold water, and let it boil. When the cherries are stoned put them into the sugar and boil them just tender, only for a few minutes, but do not let them break. After adding the cherries to the boiling sugar, stir two heaping tablespoonfuls of corn starch with a teacup nearly full of cold water; stir that into the cherries, and stir the mixture often enough to prevent burning until it has boiled sufficiently to thicken; upon cooling pour it into molds wet with cold water, and set to cool; put on ice till thoroughly cold. Serve it turned from the molds within a border of cold whipped cream.

Caramel Pudding.

One and a half pints milk, one teacupful of sugar, two tablespoonfuls corn starch, two eggs, one teaspoonful Gillett's double extract of vanilla, and pinch of salt, one teacupful brown sugar; put in a pan with a few drops of water and cook until a dark brown, and stir into the above mixture while very hot. Eat with cream.

Orange Pudding.

Four oranges, slice and sprinkle sugar over them boil one pint milk, yolks of four eggs, two tablespoonfuls corn starch, one teacupful of sugar; flavor with Gillett's double extract of vanilla. Pour over the oranges when cool, and then add the beaten whites of the eggs, with a little sugar and orange juice.

Rice Pudding No. 1.

One teacupful of uncooked rice, one quart of milk, mixed with one teacupful of cream, sugar to taste, a little salt and cinnamon; put in oven to bake about two hours, stirring occasionally.

Rice Pudding No. 2.

Take one teacupful of rice, one teacupful sugar, one teacupful of raisins, a small piece of butter, a little salt, two quarts of milk; bake from an hour and a half to two hours. Serve with sauce.

Rice Pudding No. 3.

Two teacupfuls of cold boiled rice, three eggs, one teacupful of sugar, a tablespoonful of butter, a quart of milk, a grated nutmeg, and a teacupful of raisins, stone the raisins (other flavoring may be used according to taste). Dissolve the rice in the milk, beat the eggs, add the sugar and raisins, stir all thoroughly together and bake.

Florentine Pudding.

Put a quart of milk into a pan, and let it come to a boil; mix smoothly three tablespoonfuls of corn starch and a little cold milk; add the yolks of three beaten eggs, half a teacupful of sugar, and flavoring to taste. Put this into the boiling milk and stir until of the consistency of starch ready for use, then put into the dish in which it is to be served; beat the whites of the eggs with a teacupful of pulverized sugar, spread over the top and place in the oven to brown.

Oxford Pudding.

Pare and quarter four large tart apples and boil in a very little water. Mash with a silver spoon; add one tablespoonful of butter, half a teacupful of sugar, (more if the apples are very sour), half a cup of fine breadcrumbs, the yolks of four and the whites of two eggs beaten light; put into a dish with a frosting made of the other two whites whipped stiff with sugar, and brown.

Steamed Berry Pudding.

One teacupful of sugar, two eggs, one and a half teaspoonfuls of Gillett's cream tartar baking powder, two teacupfuls of flour, one teacupful of sweet milk, two teacupfuls of berries. Steam about two hours.

Amber Pudding.

Into a quart of boiling milk stir a teacupful of cornmeal and a quart of sliced sweet apples, add a teaspoonful of salt and a teacupful of molasses. Mix thoroughly. Add two quarts of milk; pour into a large buttered dish and bake in a slow oven four hours. When cold a clear amber-colored jelly will have formed throughout the pudding, and the apples will be of a rich, dark brown.

Peach Meringue Pudding.

Stew the peaches in a syrup of sugar and water until tender, remove and boil the syrup until thick, then pour over the peaches; make a corn starch custard of the yolks of two or three eggs, about a pint of milk, two teaspoonfuls of corn starch (wet in cold milk,) sugar and vanilla. Make a meringue of the whites of the eggs and sugar and spread over the peaches. Use the custard as sauce.

Peach Cobbler.

Fill a shallow pudding dish or deep earthen pie plate with ripe peeled peaches, leaving in the pits to increase the flavor of the fruit; add cold water enough to half fill the dish, and cover the whole with a light paste rolled to twice the thickness used for pies; cut slits around the middle, prick with a fork and bake in a slow oven about three quarters of an hour. The peaches should be sugared according to taste before putting on the crust. Served either warm or cold, the crust should be inverted after being cut in sections, and the peaches piled upon it. Eat with sweet cream.

Peach Pudding.

Twelve ripe peaches, pared and stoned and stewed in a little water, one teacupful of breadcrumbs, two teacupfuls boiling milk, five tablespoonfuls sugar, five beaten eggs, a tablespoonful of butter. Soak the crumbs in the hot milk; Stir in butter, beaten eggs and sugar, at last the cooled and mashed peaches. Beat light, put in a buttered mold, set in a pan of boiling water, cover and cook an hour in a good oven. Turn out and eat with sweetened cream.

Dandy Pudding.

A tablespoonful of corn starch, stirred into a little cold milk, then add one pint boiled milk, yolks of two eggs beaten, one-quarter teacupful of sugar; beat together and place in cooking pan, then beat the whites of two eggs with one-quarter teacupful of sugar, and pour on top. Set in oven to brown.

Steamed Graham Pudding.

Two teacupfuls of graham flour, one teacupful of molasses, one teacupful of sweet milk, one teaspoonful soda, one teaspoonful salt, one tablespoonful allspice, half teacupful raisins, stoned and chopped; one and one-half hours to steam.

SAUCE.—To half teacupful of butter and one teacupful of sugar stirred to a cream, add two tablespoonfuls of milk, and let it *just come* to a boil, stir quickly and take from the fire. Should be a perfect foam.

Danish Pudding.

Two teacupfuls of breadcrumbs, one teacupful of sweet milk, two tablespoonfuls of sugar, one tablespoonful of butter; two teaspoonfuls of Gillett's baking powder, yolks of two eggs. Stir together and bake half an hour, then spread with jelly and the whites of two eggs beaten with sugar and return and bake brown.

Cottage Pudding. No. 1.

One egg well beaten, one teacupful of sugar, one teacupful sweet milk, three tablespoonfuls melted butter, one and one-half teaspoonfuls of Gillett's baking powder, two teacupfuls of flour; bake forty minutes. To be eaten with sauce.

SAUCE.—One teacupful of sugar, half teacupful of butter, half teaspoonful of salt, one tablespoonful of flour; pour on three teacupfuls of boiling water; let it boil a few minutes. Flavor with Gillett's double extract of lemon or vanilla.

Cottage Pudding. No. 2.

One egg, one teacupful of sugar, one teacupful of milk, half a teacupful of butter, two teaspoonfuls of Gillettt's baking powder, one teaspoonful of Gillett's vanilla extract, and flour enough for a common cake batter. Bake in a shallow tin, cut in pieces and serve hot with a pudding sauce.

Bread Pudding.

One pint milk, two eggs well beaten, two slices bread well buttered and cut into small squares (cut off the crust), half teacupful of cocoanut. Flavor with nutmeg, sweeten to taste; mix all together and bake. Eat with sauce. This quantity is enough for four persons.

Cake Pudding. No. 1.

Three teacupfuls flour, one teacupful sour milk, one teacupful molasses, one teacupful fruit, half tea cupful butter, one teaspoonful soda, a little salt. Steam three hours and serve with lemon sauce.

Cake Pudding.

Take pieces of dry cake of any kind, break them fine, put them with bits of butter in a bowl, make a custard of two eggs, a teacupful of cold water, half a teacupful sugar, half a teacupful of any kind of preserves or canned fruits; mix all together and pour over the cake, stir lightly and put into a buttered pudding dish. Bake until done. To be eaten with pudding sauce.

English Plum Pudding. No. 1.

Two slices of bakers' bread; soak in one pint of sweet milk, one teacupful of molasses, one egg, half teaspoonful cloves, cinnamon, allspice and mace, each, half nutmeg, quarter teaspoonful of baking soda, half pound suet chopped fine, one pound raisins, half pound currants, two ounces citron, and one pound flour. Beat well and steam five hours.

English Plum Pudding. No. 2.

Two pounds seeded raisins, two pounds currants, one pound beef suet chopped fine, six eggs, two pounds sugar, one-half pound citron, two nutmegs, one pint milk, a few breadcrumbs, and three teacupfuls of flour. Put in tin pan well greased and boil ten hours.

Date Pudding.

Six ounces suet, six ounces bread crumbs, six ounces sugar, three eggs beaten separately, two teaspoonfuls cinnamon, one-half wine glass brandy, one-half or three-quarters pound stoned dates. Beat the sugar and eggs together, stir in the other ingredients and steam two hours.

Sauce.—Beat into the yolks of three eggs enough pulverized sugar to thicken, then add one-half wine glass brandy; stir in the whites of the eggs beaten to a stiff froth.

Queen's Pudding.

One quart of milk, boil and pour over two and one-half pints of breadcrumbs, the yolks of four eggs, well beaten, a heaping tablespoonful of sugar; put in the oven and bake; then add a layer of preserves, then the whites of the eggs beaten with a teacupful of white sugar; put in the oven and brown slightly.

Mabel's Apricot Pudding.

Prepare a pint of flour as you would for biscuit, using baking powder, lard and salt, then stir in water enough to wet it so that it will spread on a tin; spread a little more than half of it on a flat tin, then cover thick with apricots that have been peeled and halved. Put the remainder of the dough on top and bake until done. It should be a light brown, to be eaten with the following

SAUCE.—Half a pint of boiling water, half a teacupful of white sugar, a pinch of salt; dissolve two teaspoonfuls of corn starch in a little water and stir into the boiling liquid, then add a tablespoonful of butter and a teaspoonful of Gillett's vanilla extract.

Bread and Butter Pudding.

Butter the slices of bread and cut them in small pieces, put a layer in the pudding dish, wash and soak for half an hour a teacupful of raisins; sprinkle a layer over the bread, then another layer of bread, and so on until the dish is full. Make a custard of a pint of milk, two eggs and half a teacupful of sugar and pour over the bread, lay bits of butter over the top. To be eaten with any pudding sauce preferred. All kinds of fruit can be used in making this pudding.

Cocoanut Pudding.

One teacupful of cold boiled rice, quarter of a pound of butter, teacupful of sugar, three eggs and half a grated cocoanut. Beat the eggs, dissolve the rice in a quart of milk, add the sugar, butter, eggs and cocoanut. Flavor to taste and bake.

Roly Poly Pudding.

Make a baking powder biscuit dough, roll it out quite thin, have it about fifteen inches long and ten inches wide; spread thickly over it any kind of fruit, either fresh, preserved or stewed; leave a space at the edge, roll up and lay in a floured cloth, pinch the edges of the pudding together, with a little flour roll the cloth loosely around it and sew the sides together; tie the ends securely, leave enough room in the cloth for the pudding to swell; put into a large kettle of boiling water and boil an hour, place a saucer or tin ring in the bottom of the kettle to prevent the pudding from burning on the bottom.

Yorkshire Pudding.

Three eggs, one pint of milk, a little salt, and flour which has been sifted twice. Beat the eggs thoroughly, add the milk and salt. Stir in the flour slowly and beat the batter until it is smooth. It should be thin enough to pour.

This pudding is to be eaten with roast beef, and should be baked with roast beef drippings over it. Grease a large dripping pan with roast beef drippings, take the roast out of the pan and hang it on the hook in the top of the oven, and place the pudding under it about half an hour before dinner time. If you have no hook in your oven or do not know how to use it, place a wire broiler over the dripping pan in which the pudding is to be baked and lay the meat on it. It is nice to have a wire cover to your dripping pan for this purpose. If you wish your pudding to be extra nice, cover the top of it with whortleberries before you put it in the oven.

Apple Dumpling.

One egg, one teacupful of milk, one tablespoonful of melted butter, two teaspoonfuls Gillett's cream tartar baking powder, flour enough to make a little thicker than batter for griddle cakes. Take teacups enough to fill steamer, butter them, then drop a tablespoonful of batter in each, fill cups nearly full of sour apples sliced thin, and cover with another tablespoonful of batter, steam half an hour. Serve with sugar and cream, or sweet pudding sauce.

Steamed Apple Dumplings.

One pound of suet, one pound of flour, one heaping teaspoonful of salt; chop suet very fine, then add the flour; mix well, add cold water enough to make a paste; add the salt, and spread thin for crust; pare ten apples, dig out center, and fill with sugar and cover with the paste; spread butter on top and lay in a steamer. Steam one hour and serve with hard sauce.

Peach Dumplings.

Peach dumplings can be made the same as apple dumplings, using twelve large peaches instead of the apples. Pare them, but do not try to take out the stone, as that spoils the peach itself.

Peach Dumplings. No. 2.

Make a light baking powder biscuit dough and roll quite thin; cut in squares about four inches; place in each square two halves of canned peaches, one tablespoonful sugar, small piece of butter, and a little juice of the fruit; pinch the corners together and place in pudding dish, the corners and edges underneath; cover them with boiling hot water; add to the water, butter, sugar, and juice from the canned fruit, and bake about twenty minutes in hot oven.

GILLETT'S MAGIC COOK BOOK.

PUDDING SAUCES.

Foamy Sauce.

Beat the whites of three eggs to a stiff froth, melt one teacupful of sugar in three tablespoonfuls of water, let it boil till it thickens, stir in one small glass of wine, then the beaten whites. Serve at once.

Brandy Sauce.

One-quarter teacupful of butter, one teacupful of sugar, beaten to a cream, add the yolks of five eggs, beaten till light, one pint of boiling water; when it thickens remove from the fire, and add two tablespoonfuls of brandy.

Banana Sauce.

Mash three large bananas in a Keystone egg-beater, then beat one teacupful of sugar into it, lastly beat in one teacupful of cream and the white of one egg. Stand in a cool place till used.

Hard Sauce.

One teacupful of sugar, three-quarters teacupful of butter beaten to a cream, add the well-beaten whites of two eggs, and one teaspoonful of Gillett's extract of vanilla. Some sprinkle nutmeg on top, but it is not always used.

Vinegar Sauce.

One teacupful of sugar, three-quarters teacupful butter, mix to a cream, one egg, one tablespoonful of vinegar; cook well in a rice boiler.

Home-Made Sauce.

One teacupful of sugar, half teacupful butter beaten to a cream, one and one-half teacupfuls of boiling water, two tablespoonfuls of corn starch (not heaping), dissolved in cold water; then stir into boiling water to cook; take off stove, stir in butter and sugar, beat well together with an egg-beater.

Good Sauce.

One teacupful of sugar, scant half teacupful of butter, one egg; rub butter and sugar to a cream, beat the egg well, stir in with butter and sugar; just before sending to table add one tablespoonful of boiling water, beat up well.

Strawberry Sauce.

Two small teacupfuls of sugar, half a teacupful of butter, beat to a cream, white of one egg beaten stiff, one teacupful of crushed strawberries, put on ice till cold.

Wine Sauce.

One teacupful of sugar, half teacupful of butter, one egg, half teacupful of wine, one teacupful of milk; mix butter and sugar to a cream; heat wine and milk separately and pour over the sugar.

Vanilla Sauce.

One egg, half teacupful of sugar, three teaspoonfuls of milk, half a teaspoonful of Gillett's extract of vanilla; beat the white of the egg to a froth; gradually beat in the sugar, add the milk, yolk and a little cream, if you have it.

Cream Sauce.

One-half teacupful of butter, one and one-half teacupfuls of sugar, one egg, one teaspoonful of boiling water, pinch of salt; beat the butter and sugar to a cream, add the yolk of the egg, then the beaten white, lastly the boiling water. Set over the teakettle ten minutes before serving.

Plain Sauce.

One-half teacupful of milk, one egg, one teacupful of sugar. Let the milk scald, add the egg and sugar, which have been well beaten with an egg-beater.

Pudding Sauce.

One teacupful of powdered sugar, yolks of two eggs; beat the eggs very light, then add the sugar, little at a time, then beat again; set in hot water until smooth and hot, then beat the whites of two eggs stiff, and stir into the yolks and sugar then pour on to one tablespoonful of brandy or wine and a small piece of butter.

DESSERT DISHES.

Gelatine Pudding.

One quart of milk, four eggs, eight tablespoonfuls of sugar, one dessertspoonful of Gillett's vanilla, half box gelatine. Beat the yolks and sugar together, and the whites to a froth; dissolve the gelatine in milk; when hot stir in sugar and yolks. Let thicken a little, then remove from the stove, cool a little, stir in beaten eggs and vanilla. Beat all thoroughly together with an egg-beater, pour in molds to cool. Eat with cream and sugar.

Snow Pudding.

Soak a half box of gelatine in a pint of boiling water, then add the juice of two lemons, and two teacupfuls of sugar. When partially cold strain; add the whites of three eggs well beaten; beat all together and set on ice. Sliced bananas, fresh strawberries, or peaches may be added, and are delicious.

CUSTARD.—One pint of milk, the well beaten yolks of three eggs, one tablespoonful of sugar, and a little salt the last thing. Flavor with Gillett's extract of almond or vanilla.

Snow Pudding. No. 2.

Pour over one-half package of Coxe's gelatine a teacupful of cold water, add one and one-half teacupfuls sugar; when soft add a teacupful boiling water and juice of one lemon, then the whites of four eggs; beat all together until it is white and frothy, or until the gelatine will not settle clear in the center of dish after standing a few minutes. Put in a glass dish, Serve with custard made from one pint milk, yolks of four eggs, four tablespoonfuls sugar, and the grated rind of one lemon; boil.

Vanilla Snow.

Cook one teacupful of rice; when nearly done add one teacupful of cream, pinch of salt, one teacupful of sugar, and the whites of two eggs, beaten; flavor with Gillett's extract of vanilla. Pile in a glass dish, put in small pieces of jelly, and eat with cream and sugar.

Spanish Cream.

Three-quarter box gelatine, one and one-half teacupfuls sugar, four eggs, one quart milk, one teaspoonful Gillett's vanilla. Soak the gelatine in milk about an hour, beat yolks and whites separately, adding half the sugar to each part. When the milk boils add the beaten yolks with the sugar added, and stir a moment, then remove from the stove, stir in the whites and flavoring. Set away in molds to cool.

Russian Cream.

One quart sweet milk, half box gelatine, yolks of four eggs, beaten to a cream with one and one-half teacupfuls of sugar. Dissolve the gelatine in milk; when heated put in sugar and eggs; boil until it curdles; while cooling beat the whites of the eggs, stir into the custard and set in molds to cool.

Russian Cream. No. 2.

One quart sweet milk, half box gelatine, yolks of four eggs beaten to a cream, with half teacupful of sugar. Dissolve the gelatine in milk on the fire; when scalded stir in eggs, boil until it curdles; while cooling beat the whites to a stiff froth and stir into the custard when partly cool.

Chantilla Cream.

Whites of two eggs, mix with one quart cream, beat to a snow, add half pound pulverized sugar. Flavor to taste and pour over sponge cake.

Orange Jelly.

Juice and rind of two oranges, juice and rind of one lemon, half box of gelatine, half teacupful sugar, one pint of boiling water. Soak the gelatine in a little cold water, add the boiling water, lemon, oranges, and sugar, strain carefully and set on ice. Half teacupful of wine may be added if you wish.

Wine Jelly.

Soak one box of gelatine together with the juice of four lemons in a pint of warm water. When dissolved add one quart of boiling water, two pounds of white sugar, one pint wine, a little cinnamon. Strain through a thin cloth and set to cool.

Wine Jelly. No. 2.

Soak a box of gelatine together with the rind and juice of three lemons, one and one-quarter pints of cold water, then add one quart of boiling water, two pounds of white sugar, one pint of port wine. Strain and set in molds to cool.

Lemon Jelly.

One box of gelatine dissolved in one pint of warm water, then add one quart of boiling water, one and one-half pints sugar; when nearly cool add the juice of three or four lemons. Strain and set to cool.

Lemon Jelly. No. 2.

Half box gelatine, 1 scant teacupful of cold water, one pint boiling water, juice of four lemons and rinds, one and one-half teacupfuls of sugar.

CUSTARD.—One pint scalded milk, four tablespoonfuls sugar, yolks of three eggs. Beat the eggs very light, last thing add pinch of salt. Flavor with Gillett's extract of lemon.

Lemon Foam.

Half ounce gelatine dissolved in a little cold water, add the yolks of six eggs well beaten, half pound powdered sugar, the juice and grated rind of three lemons. Let it stand over the fire till it thickens; beat the whites to a stiff froth, when the mixture is cold add them to it. Pour in molds and set on ice.

Lemon Foam, No. 2.

Separate the yolks of four eggs from the whites, add to the yolks one-quarter pound of sugar, the juice and rind of one lemon. Dissolve one-quarter of a teacupful of gelatine in water enough to cover. Beat all this together, then simmer over a slow fire until it thickens. When cool whip whites to a froth. Stir all together and put in a mold. Serve with whipped cream.

Floating Island.

Six eggs, one quart milk, five tablespoonfuls sugar, one teaspoonful Gillett's lemon extract. Put the milk over in a double pan, fill the lower pan with boiling water, when the milk boils stir in slowly the yolks of the eggs, which have been well beaten with the sugar, and a tablespoonful of cold milk; add the lemon and a small pinch of salt. Beat the whites of the eggs to a stiff froth with a tablespoonful of pulverized sugar; drop into the custard a tablespoonful at a time; when set take out on a platter with a perforated skimmer;

when all are cooked pour the custard into a large dish, and lay the islands on the top, or put it in the dishes in which it is to be served. To be eaten cold.

Rule for Making Custard.

A tablespoonful of sugar to each egg, and five eggs to a quart of milk is the rule always observed in making custard, etc. Always beat the yolks and whites of eggs separately, the yolks and sugar together and add the whites the last thing. With this rule for a basis a great variety of delicious custards and puddings can be made. In making boiled custards a double stew pan or two pans, one smaller than the other, should always be used. Put the water in the larger pan and when it boils place the tin containing the custard in it. To put eggs in hot milk mix the eggs first with a small quantity of cold milk, and add them gradually to the hot milk. Do not boil custards, but heat to nearly boiling point until the eggs are set. Baked custards require a moderate oven. If they are allowed to boil the milk will whey, and the custards are not nice; most puddings made of eggs and milk follow the same rule. If economy in eggs is desired, one tablespoonful of flour or heaping teaspoonful of cornstarch will be found a good substitute for an egg.

Boiled Custard.

One quart of milk, five eggs, four tablespoonfuls of sugar, a pinch of salt. Beat the eggs thoroughly, add sugar, milk and a teaspoonful of Gillett's vanilla extract; put in a pail or pan, and set in a large pan of boiling water. When set and stiff, it is done; pour into the dish in which it is to be served and sprinkle over it a tablespoonful of powdered sugar.

Baked Custard.

One quart of milk, five eggs, five tablespoonfuls of sugar, a pinch of salt; beat the eggs, stir the yolks and sugar together, add the milk and lastly the whites of the eggs. Sift over a little nutmeg and bake in a moderate oven.

Pine Apple Sponge.

Soak one-half box gelatine two hours in one-half teacupful water, to one pint can; to half can of pine apple add one teacupful of water and one teacupful of sugar (simmer fifteen minutes), add gelatine and allow to remain on stove until perfectly dissolved, then remove and place in a basin; place in a pan of cold water, add the juice of one lemon; when cold and it begins to thicken, add the stiffly beaten whites of four eggs; beat all together until it becomes liquid enough to pour into a mold. Serve next day with whipped cream or custard.

Tutti Frutti Sponge.

Prepare as for pineapple, before beating add thirty California grapes, sliced, two small bananas, three or four pears, one pint candied cherries or preserves (cherries without juice); add eggs and serve next day with ice-cream or whipped cream.

Apricot Charlotte.

Make lemon jelly as follows: Half box gelatine, one teacupful cold water, one teacupful sugar, half teacupful lemon juice, one stick of cinnamon. Soak gelatine an hour in the cold water, boil and strain, and before it gets cold, stir in apricots and put in molds. To be eaten with whipped cream.

Apple Charlotte.

Rub the bottom and sides of a baking pan with butter and line with slices of wheat bread or rolls, peel tart apples, cut small, and nearly fill the pan, scattering bits of sugar and butter between the apples; grate a small nutmeg over the apples; soak as many slices of bread or rolls as will cover, and on this put a plate with a weight on top to keep the bread close upon the apples. Bake in a quick oven. The proportion of apples, butter and sugar to be used is: To half a peck of tart apples half a pound of sugar, and a quarter of a pound of butter.

Tapioca Pudding.

Soak half teacupful of tapioca over night, then boil one quart of milk and pour over it while hot; add half a teacupful of sugar, two eggs well beaten, and a half teaspoonful of Gillett's extract of lemon, then bake; when done beat the whites of two eggs with two tablespoonfuls of sugar; spread over the top and brown a little.

Tapioca Cream.

Three heaping tablespoonfuls tapioca soaked soft in water; boil one quart milk, separate the yolks and whites of four eggs, beat the yolks and add to them one teacupful white sugar; Gillett's double extract lemon for flavoring, and the soaked tapioca; stir it all into boiling milk and let it cook a few minutes. Put the whites into the dish in which the cream is to be served, beat to a stiff froth and pour the boiling mixture into it. The beaten whites will rise to the surface. Nice either warm or cold.

Cherry Tapioca Pudding.

One teacupful of tapioca washed and soaked over night; in the morning boil in double boiler until free from lumps (it takes about two or three hours), add one teacupful of sugar, and a teaspoonful of Gillett's double extract vanilla; stone one quart cherries and sweeten. Stir the cherries into the tapioca just before serving. Serve with cream and sugar. Very nice cold.

Cherry Tapioca.

One quart of cherries, one teacupful tapioca, and a teacupful of sugar; soak the tapioca over night; let it stand on the back of the stove in the morning till the tapioca is clear. Stone the cherries, stir into the tapioca and add sugar. Turn into a dish and set on ice. This is to be eaten with sugar and cream.

Peach Tapioca.

Half teacupful tapioca, eight large peaches, teacupful of sugar. Make the same as cherry tapioca, and serve with cream and sugar.

Raspberry Tapioca.

One teacupful of tapioca. one quart box raspberries, one teacupful of sugar. Make as for cherry tapioca, serving with cream and sugar.

Strawberry Tapioca.

One teacupful tapioca, one quart fresh strawberries, sugar to taste. Make same as for cherry tapioca and serve with sugar and cream.

Orange Tapioca.

Half teacupful of tapioca, half dozen oranges sliced thin, half cup sugar. Make the same as cherry tapioca.

Apple Tapioca Pudding.

One teacupful tapioca, pour on cold water, stand on the back of the stove right after breakfast, put in the pudding dish one hour before dinner, stick quarters of apples around, a little salt.

SAUCE.—One teacupful sugar, scant half teacupful butter, one egg. Rub butter and sugar to a cream, beat egg well, stir in with the cream. Just before sending to the table, add one tablespoonful boiling water. Flavor with Gillett's Extract of Vanilla.

Hen's Nest.

Make blanc mange and set in egg shell to cool; cut lemon peel in strips the size of a straw, and boil in syrup of sugar and water until clear; make a custard and put in glass dish; put lemon peel in shape of nest; take the shells from the blanc mange and place them in the center.

Paradise Hash.

One dozen fine, large oranges; slice off the top and scoop out the inside and put in bowl; be careful not to break the skin of the orange peel. Cut in small pieces one dozen ripe bananas, can sliced pineapple cut in small pieces; put them all together, sweeten to taste, and then fill your oranges. Serve with a spoon

Dates Stuffed.

Remove the stones from one pound of fine dates by cutting sides open. Remove the shells and skins from one-half pound almonds; the skins can easily be rubbed off by first pouring boiling water upon the almond kernels. Replace the dates with almonds and arrange neatly on a dish—upon a shallow dish; dust a little powdered sugar over them and and keep them cool and dry until ready for use. Raisins can be used the same and made a very pretty table decoration.

Date Souffle.

Take a heaping teacupful of dates or prunes (if prunes, soak about one-half hour in cold water), stone them, cut up in small pieces, sprinkle two or three tablespoonfuls sugar over them, Beat the whites of five eggs to a stiff froth and sweeten with pulverized sugar; mix all together and bake a light brown. Serve cold with whipped cream sweetened and flavored.

Dessert Trifle.

Put a pint of strawberries, or any fresh fruit, in a glass dish; sprinkle with powdered sugar, then put a layer of macaroons; pour over this a custard made of one quart of milk, yolks of eight eggs, one-half teacupful sugar; heat; when cold, place the beaten whites with a half teacupful sugar on top; dot it with currant jelly when served.

Charlotte Russe.

One quart of rich cream, half a box of gelatine, two-thirds of a teacupful of milk, one teacupful of pulverized sugar, one teaspoonful of Gillett's Extract of Vanilla and the white of one egg. Put the gelatine to soak in the milk. Let it stand half an hour, while it soaks, whip the cream, which must be cold (whip it on ice if possible). Pour two-thirds of a teacupful of boiling water on the gelatine just before you finish whipping the cream, stirring it until dissolved, add the pulverized sugar, vanilla and egg beaten to a stiff foam. When the gelatine begins to thicken stir it into the cream, beat up lightly and pour into a large glass dish lined with lady fingers or sponge cake cut in slices. Keep in a cool place until served. If the cream is not rich use the whites of two more eggs.

Charlotte Russe. No. 2.

One ounce of gelatine, two tumblerfuls of milk or cream, one-half pound of powdered sugar, six eggs, Gillett's Double Extract of vanilla or almond flavoring. Soak the gelatine in the milk for fifteen minutes, and then boil until entirely dissolved. Beat the yolks of the eggs and the sugar, and stir them into the boiling mixture until it thickens like custard, then add the whites of the eggs, which must be beaten to a stiff froth, and flavor. Whip a pint of cream to a stiff froth and stir into the custard. Line a mold with sponge cake or lady fingers and fill with the mixture. Set on ice until ready for use.

Fried Apples.

Slice some apples, dip them in a batter made of on egg, sugar, milk and flour enough to thicken; fry a golden brown, sprinkle with lemon juice and serve very hot.

Raisin Puffs.

One-half teacupful of butter, two tablespoonfuls of sugar, two eggs, one teacupful of sweet milk, two teacupfuls of flour, two heaping teaspoonfuls of Gillett's baking powder, one teacupful of seeded raisins chopped fine. Steam in cups half an hour and serve with pudding sauce. This will serve nine persons.

Cream Puffs,

One teacupful of boiling water, half teacupful butter; boil both together; stir in one teacupful dry flour to the consistency of a smooth paste; remove from stove, and when partially cool stir into the mixture three eggs (not beaten); mix thoroughly for ten minutes; butter a pan, heat it; then drop in a tablespoonful at a time, leaving space between. Bake thirty minutes in a hot oven. When done make a slit in the side of each and fill with a boiled custard or charlotte russe.

Apple Lemon.

Stew half peck apples, then put in a bag and let it drip; cut up the lemons in thin pieces and soak over night in just enough water to cover it. To one cup of juice add one lemon and one cup of sugar; add the water in which the lemon is soaked; boil twenty minutes.

Apple Jelly.

Stew one-half peck apples, then put in a bag and let it drip; to one teacupful of juice add one teacupful sugar and two rose geranium leaves. Boil twenty minutes.

Coffee Jelly.

Soak one-half ounce gelatine fifteen minutes in a little water; boil one pint of coffee; pour gelatine into coffee; sweeten it to taste; strain and pour into mold; let stand two hours at least. Serve with cream.

Ginger Apples.

Pick out some hard, smooth-skinned apples, and cut them into quarters; to every pound of apples allow a quarter of a pint of water and half a pound of sugar. Boil the water and sugar together until they become a thick syrup; then pour this over the apples, allowing them to stand for twenty-four hours. Then add the same quantity of sugar as used for the syrup, and to every pound of the fruit half an ounce of bruised ginger, and a pinch of cayenne pepper tied up in muslin. Let this simmer until the fruit is transparent; add a small tablespoonful of gin, and put into jars, covering as tightly as possible. The ginger and muslin should be carefully removed.

Apple Snowballs.

Boil a quarter of a pound of rice in water until perfectly tender. Pare and core a few apples, replace the core by two cloves, brown sugar and a squeeze of lemon juice. Cover each apple with a little rice and tie it up separately in a cloth. Boil for half an hour and serve with a sweet sauce flavored with Gillett's Double Extract of lemon.

Compote of Apples.

Pare six good apples, scoop out the middles without breaking the fruit. Place in a pie dish with a quarter of a pint of water, half a pound of sugar, and the rind and juice of a half a lemon; cover the dish and cook in a hot oven until the fruit is quite tender. When done pour over the syrup, with a dessertspoonful of rum added to it, and serve with Devonshire cream.

Apples in Port Wine.

To stew apples in port wine, pare and core two pounds of sweet apples, put them into a stewpan with three wineglassfuls of port, one and one-half pounds of sugar, the rind and juice of two lemons, and cinnamon to taste. Simmer gently, removing the scum, turn the fruit with a fork from time to time without breaking them. The apples should be lifted out first, and the liquor boiled for five minutes afterward and then poured over them.

Pink Apple Snow.

Pare, core and boil six large apples to a pulp and press them through a sieve; sweeten to taste, and then to every tablespoonful of apple add a teaspoonful of currant jelly; whisk the whites of six or seven eggs with two heaping tablespoonfuls of sugar, and when frothing add them to the apple mixture, whisking all together until quite light. Pile high on a glass dish, and add a currant or strawberry jelly garniture. This dish is one very suitable for children and invalids.

Apple Float.

Take a tablespoonful of red apple or crabapple jelly to each of white of egg, and whisk until the mixture is quite light and foamy. Pour a plain custard into a deep glass dish, and pile the mixture on it. Serve with sponge rusk fingers.

CAKES AND DOUGHNUTS.

Watermelon Cake.

WHITE PART.

Two cups sugar, one cup butter, three and one-half cups flour, one cup milk, whites of eight eggs, three teaspoonfuls Gillett's baking powder.

RED PART

One cup red sugar, one-half cup butter, one-third cup milk, two cups flour, whites of four eggs, one and one-half teaspoonfuls Gillett's baking powder, one cup raisins stoned, or currants.

Be careful to keep the red part around the tube of the pan, and the white part around the edge.

Almond Cake.

Whites of six eggs, two cups sugar, one-half cup butter, two-thirds cup milk, three cups flour, two teaspoonfuls Gillett's baking powder.

FILLING.—One-half cup sugar, two eggs, three teaspoonfuls flour, or two teaspoonfuls cornstarch, one pint of milk; boil until thick,

After it has boiled add whites of two eggs well beaten, one half pound of blanched almonds.

After blanching the almonds, break half of them fine, or chop them, and put into the custard, split the rest and put on the cake after it is frosted.

Almond Cream Cake.

Whites of ten eggs, one and one-half goblets pulverized sugar, sifted, one goblet of flour, one heaping teaspoonful of cream tartar. Beat the eggs to a stiff froth, and gradually add the sifted sugar, and the flour through which has been stirred the cream tartar. Stir the mixture constantly while mixing, to prevent its being heavy, but do not beat it. Bake quickly in jelly tins.

For the cream, take one pint sweet cream, yolks of three eggs, one teaspoonful of cornstarch, one pound of chopped blanched almonds. Dissolve the cornstarch in a little milk. Heat the cream and sugar. Beat the yolks of the eggs and stir in a little of the hot cream to prevent curdling, and add to the cream with the cornstarch. Boil until thick and smooth, and lastly, stir in the chopped almonds, and when cool spread between the layers.

Chocolate Cream Cake.

Two cups sugar, one cup milk, two-thirds cup butter, three cups flour, whites of six eggs, three teaspoonfuls Gillett's baking powder.

FROSTING.—One and one-half cup granulated sugar, one-half cup milk, little of Gillett's Double Extract of Vanilla. Boil ten minutes; put in a pan of cold water and stir until cold. Spread on cake, then add melted chocolate.

Chocolate Cream Cake, No. 2.

Two cups sugar, one cup butter, one cup milk, one cup cornstarch, two cups flour, whites of six eggs, one teaspoonful soda, two teaspoonfuls cream tartar. Rub butter and sugar to a cream, add eggs well beaten, put in cornstarch dissolved in milk, stir well; cook in long, flat pan. When cold, cover with this cream, three cups granulated sugar, one cup milk, boil ten minutes, beat until cold, then put on cake and allow to cool. Melt one-fourth cake chocolate (grate and put in pan over steam), and spread over top of cream; cut in squares when cold.

Chocolate Cream Cake, No. 3.

Use the jelly cake recipe for the cake. For the cream, use one-half pound grated sweet chocolate, one coffeecup of powdered sugar, one gill of boiling milk, yolks of two eggs. Stir all together and cook to a thick cream, and spread between the layers of cake.

Chocolate Cake.

Grate one-half of Baker's chocolate, add yolk of one egg, well beaten, one-half cup of milk, one cup of sugar, and one teaspoonful of Gillett's vanilla: cook without boiling until melted, then cool. Stir one-half cup of butter and one cup of sugar to a cream, add one-half cup milk, two eggs beaten separately, two cups sifted flour, and two teaspoonfuls Gillett's Cream Tartar Baking Powder. Add the chocolate; beat well together and bake in layers, or this will make two loaves put together with boiled frosting.

FROSTING.—Two cups sugar, eight tablespoonfuls cold water, when it hairs, pour onto the beaten whites of two eggs, beat till it cools, add Gillett's Extract of Vanilla and pour over cake.

Chocolate Cake, No. 2.

Two cups sugar, two-thirds cup butter, one cup milk, three cups flour, whites of six eggs, two teaspoonfuls Gillett's baking powder; this makes two loaves.

FROSTING.—Nine tablespoonfuls or one-half cake chocolate, one and one-half cups sugar, whites of three eggs. Stir chocolate and sugar together, then add whites, frost while the cake is warm.

Chocolate Macaroons.

Three ounces of plain chocolate, one pound powdered sugar, whites of three eggs. Melt the chocolate in a pan over a slow fire, then work it to a thick paste with the sugar and eggs. Roll into cakes one-quarter of an inch thick, and cut into small cakes with round paste cutter. Butter a pan slightly and dust it with equal quantities of flour and sugar. Lay the cakes in the pan, allowing room for them to spread, and bake in a hot, but not quick, oven.

Lemon Jelly Cake.

One-half cup butter one cup sugar, one-half cup milk, two eggs, two cups flour, two teaspoonfuls Gillett's baking powder.

JELLY.—Beat one egg, add one cup of water, the grated rind and the juice of one lemon. Pour this slowly on one cup of sugar, mixed with two tablespoonfuls of flour. Cook in the double boiler till smooth, like cream.

Jelly Cake.

Three eggs, yolks and whites beaten separately, one-half cup of butter, one and one-half cups of sugar, one cup of sweet milk, three cups of sifted flour, three teaspoonfuls of Gillett's baking powder, one teaspoonful Gillett's lemon extract. Sift the flour and baking powder together. Put the ingredients together in the order given, adding the whites of the eggs last. Bake in jelly tins, in a quick oven. This will make six layers.

Jelly Roll.

Three eggs, whites and yolks beaten separately, one cup of sugar, one cup of sifted flour, two teaspoonfuls of Gillett's baking powder. Mix quickly, adding the whites of the eggs last. Bake in thin layers in square tins. While warm spread jelly on under side and roll.

Charlotte Polonaise.

Make three thick layers of cake, one gold, flavored with Gillett's lemon, and two silver with Gillett's almond. Make the cream as follows: One and one-half pints milk or cream; put over water; add the yolks of six eggs, well beaten with two tablespoonfuls arrow root. When cooked, divide into two parts; to one part add two tablespoonfuls pulverized sugar, six tablespoonfuls grated chocolate, one-forth pound crushed macaroons or cocoanut; to the second, add one dozen bitter almonds and six dozen sweet almonds, blanched and split, one ounce citron sliced thin, four tablespoonfuls pulverized sugar, one teaspoonful Gillett's extract of rose; color with cochineal coloring. Put the cakes together thus: First, a white cake with chocolate cream, then a yellow cake with rose cream, then a white cake covered with the following icing, made as follows: Whites of four eggs beaten with one pound of pulverized sugar, add, by degrees, one pound sweet almonds beaten to a paste with rose water; when nearly dry, finish with a plain white icing over top and sides. Procure the almonds ready shelled.

Dolly Varden.

One heaping cup butter, two heaping cups sugar, four eggs, two and one-half cups flour, two-thirds cup of milk, two teaspoonfuls Gillett's baking powder; put one-half of this mixture in a pan, add one tablespoonful of molasses, one large cup raisins, stoned and chopped, one-forth pound citron sliced fine, one teaspoonful cinnamon, one-half teaspoonful cloves and allspice each, grate in a little nutmeg, add one teaspoonful flour. This makes three layers. For filling, one pound raisins and one-half pound figs chopped fine, mix with jelly, water may be used.

Delicate Cake.

Two cups sugar, three-fourths cup butter, three-forths cup milk, three cups flour, whites of six eggs; two and one-half teaspoonfuls Gillett's baking powder, flavor with Gillett's vanilla.

Delicate Cake, No. 2.

Two cups of sugar, one-half cup of butter, three-fourths cup of sweet milk, three cups of flour, three teaspoonfuls of Gillett's cream tartar baking powder, one teaspoonful of Gillett's double extract of lemon, whites of six eggs. Sift the flour and baking powder together. Beat the whites of the eggs thoroughly and add the last thing. Half a cup of cornstarch in the place of flour will be found an improvement.

Coffee Cake.

Three eggs well beaten, one cup molasses, one cup sugar, one cup butter, one cup chopped raisins, one cup currants, one cup cold strong coffee, five cups flour, one teaspoonful soda, one teaspoonful cinnamon, one teaspoonful cloves, one teaspoonful nutmeg, a little salt. Bake in slow oven from one and one-half to two hours.

Coffee Cake, No. 2.

Two cups of brown sugar, one cup of butter, one cup of molasses, one cup of strong coffee, four eggs, one teaspoonful of soda, one teaspoonful of grated nutmeg, two teaspoonfuls of cloves, two teaspoonfuls of cinnamon, one pound of raisins, one pound of currants, four cups of flour. Beat the eggs until light, add the sugar and melted butter, and beat well, then add the coffee, spices and flour, and the fruit dredged with a little flour. Stir the soda into the molasses and add last, mixing thoroughly. Bake about one hour in a moderate oven, or forty minutes if baked in two loaves.

Fruit Cake, Without Butter, Eggs or Milk.

One pound of fat salt pork, two pounds of raisins, one pound of English currants, one-fourth pound of citron, one pint of molasses, one pint of boiling water, one cup of dark brown sugar, one tablespoonful each of allspice, cinnamon, mace and cloves, one grated nutmeg, and one tablespoonful of saleratus. Chop the pork until it is the same as lard, then pour the boiling water over it, only saving enough to dissolve the soda, then add the sugar, molasses and other ingredients, with the exception of the fruit, which should be added the last thing. Seed the raisins, slice the citron and wash and dry the currants and roll in flour before stirring in the cake; it should be stirred as stiff as an ordinary fruit cake; bake an hour. This will make four loaves, and will keep as long as any fruit cake.

Fruit Pound Cake.

One pound sugar, one pound currants, one pound butter, eight eggs, one-fourth pound citron, a small teaspoonful of cinnamon and allspice, three heaping teaspoonfuls of Gillett's cream tartar baking powder, one teacupful of milk, enough flour to make stiff; bake in a slow oven from an hour and a quarter to two hours.

Jersey Fruit Cake.

One and one-half teacupfuls of sugar, one-half teacupful butter, one-half teacupful sour milk, two and one-half teacupfuls flour, two teaspoonfuls Gillett's baking powder, one pound raisins, one pound currants, one fourth pound citron, four eggs.

Fruit Layer Cake.

Two teacupfuls sugar, half teacupful butter, three-quarters teacupful milk, three eggs, four teacupfuls sifted flour, two teaspoonfuls of Gillett's cream tartar baking powder; mix the ingredients in the usual way, take out one-third and add to it one teacupful of stoned raisins, one teacupful of currants, washed and dried before using, one teaspoonful of spice and one tablespoonful of molasses. Bake in layers and place between them jelly or frosting and frost the top.

Fruit Cake.

One pound of sugar, one pound butter, one and one-half pounds flour, sifted; two pounds stoned raisins, two pounds currants, three-quarters pound citron, chopped fine; ten eggs, half teacupful milk, one teacupful molasses, one teaspoonful soda, half teaspoonful cinnamon, half teaspoonful allspice, quarter teaspoonful cloves, half a nutmeg. Mix the fruit with half of the flour; cream the butter and sugar, beat the eggs until very light and add. Dissolve the soda in a little warm water and stir into the molasses, and add to the other mixture. Mix the spices with the remaining half of the flour and stir in after the milk; then add the rest of the flour and fruit, mixing thoroughly. Bake in papered tins, well buttered. This will make two loaves.

Hash Cake.

Two cups pulverized sugar, one-half cup butter, beaten to a cream; add one-half teacupful milk, two and one-half teaspoonfuls Gillett's baking powder, whites of eight eggs; bake in jelly tins. For filling, make frosting of one and one-half teacupfuls sugar, moistened with a little cold water; whites of three eggs. Add one teacupful of hickory nuts and one teacupful of raisins chopped fine.

Lady's Cake.

Three-fourths teacupful butter, two teacupfuls sugar, one-half teacupful milk, three teacupfuls flour; one teaspoonful Gillett's cream tartar baking powder, sifted with the flour, whites of six eggs, beaten to a froth. Flavor with Gillett's extract of bitter almonds.

Minnehaha Cake.

One and one-half teacupfuls granulated sugar, one half teacupful butter stirred to a cream, whites of six egg, or three whole eggs, two teaspoonfuls cream tartar stirred in two heaping teacupfuls sifted flour one teaspoonful soda in half teacupful sweet milk; bake in three layers. For filling take a teacupful sugar and a little water, boiled together until it is brittle when dropped in cold water; remove from stove and stir quickly into the well beaten white of an egg; add to this a teacupful of stoned raisins chopped fine or a teacnpful of chopped hickory nut meat, and place between layers and over top.

Improved Sunshine Cake.

The whites of seven eggs, yolks of five, one cup of granulated sugar, two-thirds cup of flour. one-third teaspoonful cream tartar, a pinch of salt, sift, measure and set aside flour, also sugar; beat yolks thoroughly, then whites, after beating a little add the cream of tartar and beat very stiff, stir in sugar lightly, then the yolks, then add flour. Put in tube pan and set in oven at once; bake from thirty-five to fifty minutes.

Scotch Cake.

Two pounds butter, four pounds flour, one pound sugar; rub thoroughly till it comes to a dough, roll out about one and one-half inches thick, pinch the edges, put in a flat pan and bake twenty minutes.

Woolly Cake.

One cup butter, one cup brown sugar, one cup molasses, one cup sour milk, four eggs, two tablespoonfuls vinegar, one teaspoonful soda, one cup chopped raisins dredged with flour, three-quarters cup flour.

Snow Ball Cake.

One cup white sugar, half cup butter, whites of five eggs, one and one-half teaspoonfuls Gillett's baking powder, flour enough to make a batter; bake in patty pans.

Cream Puffs.

Melt one-half cup of butter in one cup hot water; while boiling stir in one cup flour, remove from fire, and when cool stir in three eggs, one at a time, without beating; drop in tablespoonful on buttered pan and bake twenty-five minutes in moderate oven.

Cream for Puffs.

One-half pint of milk, one-half cup of sugar, two teaspoonfuls cornstarch, two eggs, flavor to taste, split puffs and fill with cream. This quantity will make eleven puffs.

White Fruit Cake.

Four eggs, one cup sugar, one cup butter one-half pound mixed peel, one-half pound cocoanut, one-quarter pound almonds, two teaspoonfuls Gillett's vanilla, one-half cup sweet milk, two and one-half teaspoonfuls Gillett's baking powder, add flavor the same as for an ordinary fruit cake.

White Fruit Cake, No. 2.

One cup butter, two cups sugar, two teaspoonfuls of Gillett's cream tartar baking powder, whites of five eggs, one-half pound sliced citron, two cups cocoanut, and the meats from one quart hickory nuts.

White Fruit Cake, No. 3.

One cup butter, two cups powdered sugar, three-fourths cup sweet milk, one cup raisins seeded, one-half cup citron, one-half cup blanched almonds, one teaspoonful Gillett's cream tartar baking powder, two and one-half cups of flour, eight whites of eggs, not beaten, and put in last.

Blackberry Cake.

Five eggs, two and one-half cups sugar, one and one-half cups butter, mix well together, and add two large cups of blackberry jam, one cup buttermilk, one dessertspoonful soda, four cupfuls browned flour, one teaspoonful ground cloves, one teaspoonful allspice, one tablespoonful cinnamon, one and one-half pound citron.

Bride's Loaf.

Stir to a cream two cups powdered sugar and three-fourths cup butter, add one cup milk, two cups flour mixed well with one cup cornstarch and three teaspoonfuls Gillett's cream tarter baking powder, whites of six eggs well beaten, flavoring to taste, bake in moderately heated oven. When cold ice with the whites of two eggs beaten stiff with powdered sugar, and one teaspoonful cornstarch.

Brod Torte.

Six ounces grated almonds, twelve yolks of eggs, three-fourths pound sugar, the grated rind of a lemon, little less than an ounce cinnamon and cloves mixed, five ounces of finely grated pumpernickel, and the whites of ten eggs beaten to a stiff foam. The twelve, yolks, the almonds and sugar must be stirred one-half hour, then the bread added, and lastly the whites of the eggs. Take from one to one and one-half hours to bake, with most heat underneath, till it has raised, with a moderate heat all the time. Pumpernickel can be bought at any bakery.

Buttermilk Cake.

Two cups sugar, one teaspoonful cinnamon, one teaspoonful cloves, one-half nutmeg (grated), two cups buttermilk, one teaspoonful soda, one cup chopped raisins, enough flower to stiffen.

Short Cake, Strawberry.

Two thirds cup milk, one-half cup sugar (small)' two cups flour, one large tablespoonful butter, two teaspoonfuls Gillett's cream tarter baking powder, one egg well beaten. Melt the butter, beat with the sugar, add the egg and milk, then lastly the baking powder and flour. Split in half and heap with strawberries and sugar.

Orange Cake.

Two cups sugar, one-half cup butter, three and one-half cups sifted flour, one and one-half cups sweet milk, three eggs beaten separately, two teaspoonfuls Gillett's cream tartar baking powder. Bake in four jelly tins.

JELLY.—Juice and grated rind of two oranges, two tablespoonfuls cold water, two cups sugar, set in pot of boiling water, and when scalding hot stir in the yolks of two well beaten eggs, and just before taking from the fire stir in the beaten white of one egg. When cold put between layers of cake; frost top with other egg, two layers for loaf.

Silver Cake.

Two cups of sugar, one-half cup of butter, three-fourths cup of sweet milk, two and one-half cups of flour, two teaspoonfuls of cream tartar, one teaspoonful soda, eight eggs (whites), flavor to taste.

Silver Cake, No. 2.

Silver cake No. 2 can be made with the recipe for Gold Cake, using one cup of butter and scant measure of flour, sweet or sour milk as preferred. This may be baked in separate cakes or a spoonful of the gold and silver parts may be put alternately in a pan and baked like marble cake.

Iowa Cake.

One and one-half cups of sugar, one-half cup of butter, one-half cup of sweet milk, two cups of flour, twelve eggs (yolks), one teaspoonful of cream tartar, one half teaspoonful of soda, flavor to taste.

Caramel Cake.

Eight eggs (whites) beaten stiff, two cups pulverized sugar, one-half cup of butter; one-half cup sweet milk, two and one-half cups of flour, two teaspoonfuls of Gillett's cream tartar baking powder, (or two teaspoonfuls of cream tartar and one of soda). Bake in eight layers, or in one square loaf, fill and frost with the following caramel: One cup granulated sugar, three tablespoonfuls of water, put in frying pan and stir constantly till burned a dark brown, then pour in hot water till it is the consistency of syrup, use it to color and flavor your boiled icing, for which take one large cup of granulated sugar, one-fourth cup of water, boil till it hairs, turn slowly onto the beaten white of one egg, then add enough of the browned sugar to make it a nice color and taste.

Caramel Cake, No. 2.

Two cups of sugar, three-fourths cup of butter, one cup of milk, one cup of cornstarch, two cups sifted flour, two teaspoonfuls of Gillett's cream tartar baking powder, whites of seven eggs, bake in a shallow pan. For the caramel frosting, take one cup of brown sugar, one-half cup of milk, butter the size of an egg, scant quarter of a pound of chocolate, two teaspoonfuls Gillett's extract vanilla. Boil until thick, like syrup, spread on the cake and set in the oven to dry.

Vermont Pork Cake.

One-half pound fat salt pork chopped fine, one cup of sugar, one cup of molasses, one cup of milk, three and one-half cups of flour, one teaspoonful of soda, spices and fruit to taste.

Wedding Cake.

One pound of fine sugar, one pound of butter, one-half pound of citron chopped fine, one-half pound of currants, one pound of raisins seeded and chopped, one pound of flour sifted twice, twelve eggs, two tablespoonfuls of nutmeg, one tablespoonful each of cloves and cinnamon. Cream the butter and sugar, add the beaten yolks of the eggs, and half the flour; stir well before adding the spices, the well beaten whites of the eggs and the rest of the flour; dredge the fruit and add last; bake three hours in a slow oven.

Sponge Cake.

Five eggs, one-half pound sugar, one-half pound flour, one teaspoonful of Gillett's cream tartar baking powder, sifted with the flour, grated rind and juice of one lemon. Beat the yolks of the eggs and the sugar until perfectly light, gradually add the flour, then whites of the eggs and lemon. Bake in a moderate oven.

Sponge Cake, No. 2.

Three eggs, one and one-half cups of white sugar, two cups of flour, one-half cup of cold water, two teaspoonfuls of Gillett's cream tartar baking powder. Sift the flour and baking powder together, beat the eggs one minute, add the sugar and beat five minutes, add one cup of flour, beating one minute, then add the water and the rest of the flour and any desired flavoring, and beat one minute; bake in a slow oven.

Velvet Sponge Cake.

Two teacupfuls sugar, six eggs, leave out whites of three, one teacupful boiling water, two and one-half teacupfuls sifted flour, one tablespoonful Gillett's cream tartar baking powder, and sift it several times with the flour. Beat yolks, then add sugar and beat fifteen minutes, add the beaten whites, and the cup of boiling water just before the flour, flavor and bake in four layers in biscuit tins. Use two layers for a cake.

Angel Food Cake.

One and one-half coffeecups of sugar, one coffee-cup of sifted flour, one teaspoonful each of cream tartar and Gillett's double extract vanilla, whites of eleven eggs. Sift the flour five times, adding the cream tartar before the last sifting; sift the sugar (granulated) five times; beat the whites of the eggs on a platter till they form a stiff froth; add the sugar lightly, and then slowly stir in the flour, lastly the vanilla, stirring constantly until the cake is put into the pan, which should be new, never having been greased. Bake forty minutes in a moderate oven, which should not be opened until the cake has been in fifteen minutes. Turn the pan upside down to cool.

Bread Cake.

One cup of granulated sugar; one cup of yeast bread dough, one-half cup of butter, scant, one-quarter teaspoonful soda dissolved in a tablespoonful of sour milk, one egg, spices to taste. Stir all together; add enough flour to make a stiff cake dough and work with the hands until the other ingredients are well mixed with the light dough. Add one-half cupful each of raisins and currants; let it rise half an hour in the pans in which it is to be baked, and bake in a moderate oven.

Bread-batter Cake.

Three cups of light bread-batter, two cups of sugar, one cup of butter, two eggs. Stir all well together and let it rise for half an hour, after which bake in a quick oven.

Currant Cake.

Five cups of flour, three cups of sugar, one and one-half cups of butter, one-half cup sweet milk, six eggs, one nutmeg, three-fourths pound of currants, three teaspoonfuls Gillett's cream tartar baking powder. Put the ingredients together in the usual way, dredge the currants with flour before using. Bake two hours in a moderate oven.

Plain Cake.

Three eggs, one and one-half cups of sugar, one-half cup butter, one-half cup milk, three cups of flour sifted before measuring, two teaspoonfuls Gillett's cream tartar baking powder, one-half nutmeg, rose-water to taste. Sift the flour and baking powder together. Put the ingredients together in the order given and bake in a steady oven forty minutes.

Pound Cake.

One pound of sugar, one-half pound of butter, one pound sifted flour, one-half cup of sweet milk, six eggs, one half teaspoonful soda, one teaspoonful cream tartar, flavor to taste. Mix the cream tartar with the flour, cream the butter and sugar, add the yolks of the eggs and the milk, and gradually stir in the flour; dissolve the soda in a little of the milk and beat thoroughly into the mixture, adding the well-beaten whites of the eggs last. Bake in a quick oven.

Cocoanut Pound Cake.

One-half pound of butter, one pound of flour, one pound powdered sugar, one cup of milk, five eggs, one-fourth pound of prepared cocoanut, two teaspoonfuls of Gillett's cream tartar baking powder, one teaspoonful Gillett's double extract lemon, a little salt. Stir the butter to a cream and add the beaten yolks of the eggs, sugar, milk, and flour with which the baking powder has been sifted. Stir in the well-beaten whites of the eggs, and lastly add the cocoanut and the lemon extract. Pour into pan lined with buttered paper, and put into a moderately cool oven, with a gradual increase of heat. When done spread with icing, while both are warm.

Gold Cake.

Two cups of sugar, three-fourths cup of butter, one cup sour milk, four cups flour, one teaspoonful of soda, yolks of eight eggs, one tablespoonful of cornstarch, lemon or vanilla flavoring, sweet milk and three teaspoonfuls of Gillett's cream tartar baking powder may be used instead of the sour milk and soda.

Nut Cake.

One and one-half cups of sugar, one-half cup of butter, three-fourth cup of sweet milk, two cups of sifted flour, whites of four eggs, two teaspoonfuls of Gillett's cream tartar baking powder. Mix the flour and baking powder together; beat the whites of the eggs stiff and add last to the other ingredients. Lastly stir in one large cupful of chopped hickory nut meats, and bake in a square loaf. Frost the top when done.

Banana Cake.

Two eggs, one cup of sugar, one-third cup of butter, one half cup of milk, one and three-fourths cups sifted flour, three teaspoonfuls of Gillett's cream tartar baking powder. Mix the baking powder well with the flour, cream the butter and sugar, add the well-beaten eggs, milk, and stir the flour in gradually. Bake in layers; when done frost each layer, and cover with sliced bananas; frost the top.

Brooklyn Cake.

One-half cup of lard, one-half cup of butter, one cup of sugar, one cup of molasses, one-half cup of sour milk, one scant teaspoonful of soda, three eggs, one teaspoonful each of cinnamon, cloves and nutmeg, three cups of sifted flour. Beat the sugar and eggs well together, add the melted lard and butter, then the molasses, flour and spices, and lastly the sour milk and soda, which should be thoroughly mixed. Bake about forty minutes in a moderately hot oven.

New Year's Marble Cake.

WHITE PART.—One cup of white sugar, one-half cup of butter, one half cup sweet milk, two and one-half cups of sifted flour, two teaspoonfuls of Gillett's cream tartar baking powder, mixed with the flour, whites of four eggs well-beaten and added last, one-half teaspoonful of Gillett's vanilla.

DARK PART.—Yolks of four eggs, one cup of brown sugar, one-half cup of molasses, one-half cup of butter, one-half cup of sour milk, two and one-half cups sifted flour one teaspoonful of soda, one teaspoonful each of cloves and cinnamon, one-half teaspoonful of allspice, one nutmeg. For the white part, mix the ingredients in the order given. For the dark part, beat the eggs, add the sugar, butter, molasses, flour and spices, and lastly the sour milk into which has been stirred the soda. Put the two parts into the cake pans by spoonfuls, the light and dark alternately, or in layers, with the dark layer on the top; frost. Currants or raisins may be added to the dark part if desired. Bake slowly.

Fig Cake.

One-half cup of butter, one-half cup of milk, one heaping coffeecup sugar, three cups of flour, two small teaspoonfuls of Gillett's cream tartar baking powder sifted with the flour, whites of eight eggs, three-fourths pound of figs. Sift the flour before measuring, and again after adding the baking powder. Cut up the figs, dredge with flour, and add last.

Fig Layer Cake.

Two eggs, one cup of sugar, one-half cup of milk, one large heaping cupful of sifted flour, one and one-half teaspoonfuls of Gillett's cream tartar baking powder, butter the size of an egg. Stir the butter and sugar to a cream, add the yolks of the eggs, milk and the flour, which should be sifted again after adding the baking powder, and lastly the beaten whites of the eggs. Bake quickly in jelly tins; this will make three layers. Chop one-half pound of figs, and cook in one teacupful of water and two-thirds cup of white sugar, until soft and smooth. When cool place this between the layers and frost the top with white frosting.

Cup Cake.

Three cups of sugar, one cup of butter one cup of milk, four cups of flour, four eggs, two teaspoonfuls of Gillett's cream tartar baking powder. Cream the butter and sugar well, then add eggs, milk and flour, with which the baking powder has been sifted. Bake quickly in molds or in a loaf, as preferred.

Cream Cake.

Two eggs, one cup of sugar, one cup of cream, two cups of flour, one-half teaspoonful of soda. Beat the eggs and sugar well together, add the flour and then the cream, into which the soda has been stirred. Flavor to taste and bake in a loaf or in layers, about twenty minutes.

Every-day Cake.

One cup of molasses, one cup of sugar, one cup of butter, two-thirds cup of milk, two eggs, three teaspoonfuls of Gillett's cream tartar baking powder, one teaspoonful each of cloves, cinnamon and nutmeg, a small pinch of salt, three cups of flour, sifted before measuring. Bake about forty minutes.

Composition Cake.

Five cups of sifted flour, two cups of butter, three cups of sugar, one cup milk, five eggs, three teaspoonfuls of Gillett's cream tartar baking powder. Sift the flour before measuring it and again after adding the baking powder, beat the yolks of the eggs, butter and sugar until light, add the milk and flour, and lastly the well-beaten whites of the eggs. Use any desired flavoring; bake slowly. This is very excellent.

Ribbon Cake.

Two cups of sugar, two-thirds cup of butter, one cup of milk, four scant cups of sifted flour, four eggs, two teaspoonfuls of Gillett's cream tartar baking powder, one teaspoonful of Gillett's double extract of lemon; divide the mixture and to one-half add two teaspoonfuls cinnamon, one cup of currants, and one-eighth pound citron. Bake in layers, and when done arrange the light and dark layers alternately, putting either jelly or frosting between them, and frosting on top.

Cream Layer Cake.

For the cake, use the recipe given for Fig Layer Cake.

CREAM.—One-half pint of milk; one half cup of sugar, one egg, a very small piece of butter, one tablespoon of flour or cornstarch wet in a little milk, flavor to taste. Let the milk come to a boil, add the sugar, butter, flour (or cornstarch), and lastly the beaten egg, into which has been stirred a little hot milk to prevent curdling. Cook about two minutes, when nearly cold, flavor, and place between the layers.

Cookies.

Two cups sugar, one cup of shortening (one-half cup butter and one-half cup lard), one-half cup sour milk, two eggs, one teaspoonful saleratus, and enough flour to make this stiff enough.

Cookies, No. 2.

Two cups of sugar, one cup of butter, one cup of milk, three eggs, two teaspoonfuls Gillett's cream tartar baking powder. Use flour enough to make a soft dough; roll thin, sift over with sugar, and bake in a quick oven.

Almond Cookies.

One-half pound sugar, one-half pound butter, four eggs, nine ounces flour, two teaspoonfuls Gillett's baking powder. Bake in very thin sheets, before being put in the oven, sprinkle with sugar and sliced almonds. Almonds may be grated or pounded if preferred

Cocoanut Cookies.

One cup sugar, one-half cup butter, one cup grated cocoanut, one egg, one-half teaspoonful of soda, flour enough to make a dough that can be rolled out thin; bake in a quick oven.

Caraway Cookies.

Two cups of sugar, one-half cup of butter, one cup of sweet milk, one teaspoonful of Gillett's cream tartar baking powder, caraway seeds, flour enough to roll out. These are deliciously light and tender.

Ginger Cookies.

One pint of New Orleans molasses, one-half cup of brown sugar, two-thirds cup of shortening, one teaspoonful of ginger, one-half cup of hot water, and one tablespoonful of soda. Mix stiff enough to roll nicely, but not too stiff, bake in hot oven.

Cocoanut Drops.

One-half pound grated cocoanut, one-half pound of powdered sugar, whites of four eggs, one teaspoonful of Gillett's double extract lemon. Beat the eggs and sugar until light and white, then add the lemon, and as much cocoanut as will make it as thick as can be easily stirred with a spoon. Drop on greased paper and bake.

Hermits.

Two cups brown sugar, two-thirds cup butter, two eggs, one teaspoonful soda, spice with cinnamon, cloves and nutmeg; flour till stiff enough to roll out, two cups chopped currants and raisins.

Hermits, No. 2.

One cup sugar, one-half cup molasses, two-thirds cup of currants, two eggs, six tablespoonfuls sweet milk, one teaspoonful each of cinnamon and cloves, one teaspoonful soda, flour enough to roll.

Sunshines.

One egg, one tablespoonful sugar, stiffen with flour same as for noodles, roll very thin, cut in diamonds or squares and fry quickly in clean lard, sprinkled with pulverized sugar while warm.

Hound's Ears or Magic Pastry.

Two tablespoonfuls of white powdered sugar, four ounces fine flour, two eggs; mix all together very smoothly; cut in leaf shape and fry in lard.

Crinkles.

One pound flour, or three and one-fourth cupfuls, one-half pound butter, or one cupful; one-half pound sugar, or one cupful; eight hard boiled eggs (yolks), one raw yolk. Cut out with a doughnut cutter; after rolling about as thin as you would for cookies, rub the top with the white of egg, and then sprinkle with chopped almonds.

Ginger Snaps.

One cup sugar, one cup molasses, one cup of shortening (half butter and half lard), mix this and let it just come to a boil; when cool put in one teaspoonful of ginger, one teaspoonful of soda dissolved in hot water, then put flour enough so they will not be sticky but will roll out as soft as possible.

Ginger Snaps, No. 2.

One cup of molasses, one-half cup of butter, one teaspoonful of soda, one tablespoonful of ginger, flour enough to make a stiff dough. Roll as thin as possible.

Ginger Snaps, No. 3.

Two cups of molasses, one cup of brown sugar, one cup of butter or lard, one teaspoonful of soda, one tablespoonful ginger. Dissolve the soda in a very little hot water. Mix stiff with flour and roll out thin.

Ginger Drop Cookies.

Three eggs, one cup of brown sugar, one cup of molasses, one cup of lard or butter, one tablespoonful of ginger, one large teaspoonful of soda, one cup of boiling water, five cups of flour. Dissolve the soda in the boiling water, and add the last thing; mix stiff and roll out.

Corn Starch Patties.

One pound Kingsford's cornstarch, one pound sugar; one-half pound butter, six eggs, two teaspoonfuls Gillett's cream tartar baking powder, Gillett's extract vanilla; beat well together; bake in patty pans.

Velvet Cakes.

Three cups of sugar, one cup of butter, beaten to a cream, the whites and yolks of six eggs, well-beaten, two tablespoonfuls sweet milk, one half teaspoonful cream tartar, one-quarter teaspoonful soda sifted with one pound cornstarch, one teaspoonful lemon juice; bake in patty pans.

Jumbles.

Two cups of sugar, one cup of butter, one-half cup of sweet milk, two eggs, a little nutmeg, one-half teaspoonful of soda. Cream the butter and sugar, beat the eggs very light and add. Dissolve the soda in the milk, and add enough flour to roll into cakes, handling as light as possible. Bake in a quick oven.

Jumbles, No. 2.

One cup of butter, one cup of sugar, two cups of flour, four eggs, one-half teaspoonful of Gillett's cream tartar baking powder. Cream the butter and sugar, add the well-beaten eggs, then the flour; roll out and cut with jumble cutter of any desired shape, and bake in a quick oven.

Soft Gingerbread.

Two and one-half cups sifted flour, one cup sour milk, one cup brown sugar (or white), one cup molasses (N. Orleans), one-half cup butter, two eggs, one heaping teaspoonful soda, ginger and spices, one teaspoonful of each; bake twenty minutes.

Soft Gingerbread, No. 2.

One cup molasses, one cup sugar, one cup boiling water, two eggs, two teaspoonfuls ginger, one teaspoonful soda, three cups flour, one cup butter; beat butter, sugar and molasses, add water, then eggs last of all.

Soft Gingerbread, No. 3.

One cup molasses, one cup sour milk, one cup sugar, two-thirds cup butter, two and one-half cups flour, one teaspoonful soda, one teaspoonful ginger, one teaspoonful each of all spices, two eggs.

Poor Man's Soft Gingerbread.

One teaspoonful soda dissolved in one cupful of molasses, add two tablespoonfuls butter, one-half cnp sour milk, one teaspoonful ginger, one and one-half cups flour.

Honeycomb Gingerbread.

One pound molasses, one-half pound butter, one-half pound flour, ginger to taste. Spread thin as possible on tins, when baked cut in strips and roll.

Doughnuts.

Four eggs, eight tablespoonfuls sugar, half a cup of milk, one-quarter cup of butter, pinch of salt, half a teaspoonful soda, flavor with one nutmeg, and flour enough to roll out.

Bread Doughnuts.

Take three cups bread dough, one cup sugar, one egg, butter the size of an egg, salt; mix together and set to rise; when risen pull out with the hands until the dough is very light; break off pieces with the hands and drop into hot lard and fry; sprinkle with sugar or cinnamon.

Crullers.

One-half cup sugar, one cup milk, two eggs, two teaspoonfuls Gillett's baking powder, one tablespoonful melted butter, nutmeg to taste; fry in hot lard.

One Egg Crullers.

One cup sugar, one cup buttermilk, or sour milk, one egg, three tablespoonfuls melted butter, one teaspoonful soda, flavor with nutmeg, add a pinch of salt; mix soft as possible, and cut in any desired shape. Have ready a kettle of hot fat; brown quickly on one side, turn, and drain on a piece of brown paper.

Cream Fritters.

One cup of cream, whites of five eggs well-beaten, two cups of flour, pinch of salt, flavor with nutmeg; stir the whites into the cream, add the flour, nutmeg and salt, and beat thoroughly a few minutes. This makes a thick batter, drop a spoonful at a time in hot lard. Drain and serve with jelly or sauce. Pull open, as it hurts them to use a knife.

Apple Fritters.

Make a batter one cup of milk, two cups of flour, one heaping teaspoonful of Gillett's cream tartar baking powder, two eggs beaten separately, pinch of salt, and a tablespoonful of sugar. Warm the milk, add the yolks well-beaten, and the sugar, then the flour with the baking powder sifted in, and the beaten whites, stir well and add slices of sour apples, being careful to get the batter all over them, drop by spoonfuls in hot lard and fry. Serve with maple syrup.

Banana Fritters.

Peel the bananas, cut them in slices, and cover with the batter used in Apple Fritters, and fry in hot lard. Drain and serve with maple syrup.

Peach Fritters.

Peel the peaches, split in two and remove the stones, sprinkle powdered sugar over them, dip each piece in batter and fry in hot lard.

Pineapple Fritters.

Make the same batter as for Apple Fritters, pare the pineapple, cut in slices, then halve them, dip into the batter, fry and drain as in the preceding recipe.

Orange Fritters.

Orange fritters can be made the same as Pineapple Fritters, first slicing the oranges and sprinkling them with powdered sugar, then covering with batter.

Queen Fritters.

Use the recipe for Cream Puffs, also the filling. (See cream puff recipe). Drop a spoonful of the batter into the hot lard, turn, and drain; then sprinkle with powdered sugar and let cool; open one side with a sharp knife, put a spoonful of the filling into it, and serve cold.

Parsnip Fritters.

Boil four good sized parsnips until tender, mash, and season with salt, pepper and a little butter. Drop a little of this at a time into the batter and cover well, then drop into hot lard and fry light brown.

Dwight's Cow Brand Soda Recipes

Neapolitan Cake.

DARK.—One cupful of brown sugar, two eggs, half cup of butter, half cup of molasses, half cup of strong coffee, half cup of flour, one cup of seeded raisins, one cup of currants, one cup of citron cut fine, one teaspoonful of cinnamon and cloves, one teaspoonful of Dwight's Cow Brand Soda.

LIGHT.—Two cups of white sugar, half cup of butter, one cup of milk, two and one-half cups of flour, three-fourths cup of cornstarch, whites of four eggs, two teaspoonfuls of Gillett's cream tartar baking powder, flavor to taste with Gillett's double extract lemon. Bake in layers in a square pan and put together with icing.

White Fruit Cake.

One pound of white sugar, one pound of flour, half pound of butter, whites of twelve eggs, two pounds of citron cut in thin long strips, two pounds of blanched almonds cut in strips, one large grated cocoanut. Before the flour is sifted, add one teaspoonful of Dwight's Cow Brand Soda, two teaspoonfuls of cream tartar. Cream the butter as you do for pound cake, add the sugar and beat it a while, then add the whites of the eggs and flour, and after beating sufficiently, add about one-third of the fruit, adding the rest in layers with the batter. Bake slowly same as other fruit cake.

Blueberry Cake.

One pint flour, one teaspoonful Dwight's Cow Brand Soda, two teaspoonfuls pure cream tartar, two eggs, one-half pint milk, one pint of blueberries.

Healthful Shortcake.

One pint rich sour buttermilk, one quart strawberries, one teaspoonful Dwight's Cow Brand Soda, a little salt, Graham flour. To the milk add soda, salt and sufficient Graham flour to make a tolerably stiff batter; bake this in two pans (as for jelly cake) in a brisk oven; have ready the strawberries, or any kind of fruit desired, mashed and sweetened to taste. When the cakes are baked, split and butter them, spread upon the halves the prepared fruit and put them together again. This may be eaten either hot or cold, and with cream.

Cocoanut Cake.

One cup of fresh butter, three cups of white sugar, three and one-half cups of flour, one cup of sweet milk, one teaspoonful of Dwight's Cow Brand Soda, and two of pure cream tartar, whites of ten eggs; bake in cakes an inch thick. Icing, one large grated cocoanut, and whites of four eggs beaten to a stiff froth. To make one of the yellows, take three cups of sugar, three and one-half cups of flour, one cup of sweet milk, one teaspoonful of Dwight's Cow Brand Soda, and two of pure cream tartar. This makes very good jelly cake, or gems.

Loaf Cocoanut Cake.

One grated cocoanut, one cup of butter, three of sugar, one of milk, four and a half of flour, four eggs, one teaspoonful of Dwight's Cow Brand Soda, and two teaspoonfuls of pure cream tartar.

Marble Cake.

WHITE.—One cup of butter, one of cream or sweet milk, two of white sugar, four of flour, whites of eight eggs, and two teaspoonfuls of Gillett's cream tartar baking powder; flavor with Gillett's double extract lemon.

BLACK.—Half cup of butter, half cup of sour milk, one cup of brown sugar, half cup of New Orleans molasses, three cups of flour, yolks of four eggs and one whole one added, one teaspoonful of Dwight's Cow Brand Soda, half teaspoonful each of cloves, cinnamon, allspice and nutmeg, a small wineglassful of brandy. Put in pan in alternate layers, using a smaller portion of white than of black.

Blackberry Jam Cake.

One cup of sugar, three-fourths cup of butter, one and one-half cups flour, three eggs, three tablespoonfuls of sour cream, one teaspoonful Dwight's Cow Brand Soda, one cup of blackberry jam, nutmeg, cinnamon and allspice to taste. Stir all together and bake in biscuit pan and spread with icing; or bake in layers and put together with icing.

Perfection Cake.

One and a half cups sugar, half cup of butter, half cup of milk, two cups of flour, whites of six eggs, one teaspoonful of pure cream tartar in the flour, and a half teaspoonful of Dwight's Cow Brand Soda in the milk; add to it the sugar and butter, well-beaten together, then the milk and soda, flour and whites of eggs.

Fruit Cake.

One pound of granulated sugar, one pound of butter, one pound of flour, two pounds of raisins, two pounds of currants, half pound of citron, one cup of brown sugar, one cup of molasses with one teaspoonful of Dwight's Cow Brand Soda dissolved in it, one cup of strong, clear coffee, ten eggs beaten separately, one grated nutmeg, one dessertspoonful of cinnamon, and very little allspice. Wash and dry currants, seed raisins and chop half. Bake slowly four hours with a pan of water in the oven.

Sponge Cake.

Three eggs, beat two minutes, add one and one-half cups white sugar and beat five minutes; one cup flour beat two minutes, another cup of flour with one teaspoonful pure cream of tartar stirred in one-half cup cold water with one-half teaspoonful Dwight's Cow Brand Soda, little salt and flavor. Makes two loaves.

Sponge Cake.

Three eggs, one cup sugar, one-half teaspoonful Dwight's Cow Brand Soda, one teaspoonful pure cream tartar, one cup flour. Beat the yolks and whites separately, then beat in sugar, dissolve soda in a little water, add to the egg and sugar, then add pure cream of tartar to the flour, then mix altogether and bake.

Jelly Roll.

Three eggs, one cup sugar, one cup flour, one teaspoonful pure cream tartar, one-half teaspoonful Dwight's Cow Brand Soda, one-half teaspoonful Gillett's double extract lemon. Sift pure cream tartar with the flour, dissolve the soda in a very little water. Bake in dripping pan, spread with jelly while hot and roll.

Lady Fingers.

One cup sugar, one-half cup butter, one quarter cup milk, one egg, one pint flour, one teaspoonful pure cream tartar, one-half teaspoonful Dwight's Cow Brand Soda. Cut into little strips, roll with your hands in sugar and bake in a quick oven.

Snow Flake Cake.

One-half cup butter, one and one-half cups sugar, two cups pastry flour, one quarter cup milk, five eggs (whites only), one teaspoonful pure cream tartar, one-half teaspoonful Dwight's Cow Brand Soda, juice of half a lemon. Beat the butter to a cream, gradually add the sugar, then the lemon, and when very light the milk; next the whites of the eggs, beaten to a stiff froth, then the flour in which the soda and cream of tartar are well mixed. Bake in sheets in a moderate oven; when nearly cold, frost.

FROSTING.— Three eggs (whites), two large cups powdered sugar, one-half grated cocoanut, juice of half a lemon. Add the sugar gradually to the whites, already beaten to a stiff froth; then the lemon and cocoanut. Frost the top of each loaf, or make layer cake of it by putting the sheets together.

Sunshine Cakes.

Yolks of eleven eggs, one cup butter, two and one-half cups flour, one-half teaspoonful Dwight's Cow Brand Soda; two cups sugar, one cup milk, one teaspoonful pure cream tartar, flavor with Gillett's double extract vanilla.

FROSTINGS AND FILLINGS FOR CAKES.

Rocky Mountain Filling.

One fresh cocoanut, one cup raisins, quarter pound citron, half pound almonds, one pound dates, six large figs, half cup currants; make a thin icing of whites of three eggs and two cups sugar; ice both sides of each of your layers; prepare the fruit as follows: Grate the cocoanut; take one-third of the almonds, blanched, and chop fine with all of the fruit, mix with a small part of the cocoanut after icing the cakes; spread the mixture on each layer, and sprinkle with cocoanut on top layer, spread fruit and use the whole almonds for decoration, sprinkling with the cocoanut.

Orange Filling

Boil to a syrup one cup sugar, four tablespoonfuls water, add the well-beaten whites of two eggs, beat until somewhat cool, then add the grated half of peel and pulp of orange.

Raisin Filling.

One cup chopped seeded raisins, one cup chopped nuts, one cup sugar dissolved; stir in raisins and nuts while boiling; white of one egg beaten and stirred in when taken off the stove.

Chocolate Filling.

Two cups grated chocolate, one cup sugar, one cup water, small piece of butter, boil until it begins to thicken, flavor with Gillett's double extract vanilla.

Fig Filling.

One-half pound figs chopped fine, quarter pound almonds chopped fine, add one large cup water with half cup sugar; cook until it thickens somewhat; put in filling when nearly cold.

Filling for Fig Cake.

One-fourth pound chopped figs, and one-fourth pound chopped raisins, three or four tablespoonfuls sugar, add boiling water until it is thick enough.

Fig Filling Without Almonds.

One-half pound figs chopped fine, one cup water, half cup sugar; cook until soft and thickens.

Lemon Jelly Filling.

Grate the rind of one lemon, add juice and large spoonful of water, half cup sugar, butter the size of walnut, one egg, beat all and let boil a few minutes.

Almond Nougat Filling.

One pound sweet almonds, blanched and chopped, one cup sour cream, one cup sugar, flavor with Gillett's double extract vanilla; beat all together and spread between layers.

Almond Filling.

Whip thick cream, sweaten a little, add chopped almonds or other nut meats, mix well and spread.

Caramel Filling.

Three cups light brown sugar, three-quarters cup butter, half cup cream, one teaspoonful Gillett's double extract vanilla; stir well and boil in double pail fifteen minutes; take from stove and beat until cold; spread between layers.

Cream Filling.

One pint milk, two tablespoonfuls cornstarch, yolks of two eggs, three tablespoonfuls sugar, flavoring to taste; boil until thick.

Yellow Frosting.

Yolks of three eggs beaten light, with one and one-half cups sugar, flavor with Gillett's double extract vanilla. A tablespoonful of sweet cream or one of vinegar will prevent crumbling.

Boiled Frosting.

One cup sugar, four tablespoonfuls cold water; when it hairs, pour over the beaten white of one egg, beat till it cools.

Maple Sugar Frosting.

Make same as Boiled Frosting, using maple sugar instead of granulated.

Milk Frosting.

Half cup milk, one and one-half cups sugar; let it boil until it begins to thicken, then stir in a cup of chopped raisins, figs, dates or chocolate.

Chocolate Frosting.

Nine tablespoonfuls or half cake chocolate, one and one-half cups sugar, whites of three eggs; stir chocolate and sugar together, then add whites, beat till it gets cold.

Caramel Frosting.

One cup milk, three-fourths cup of butter; melt the butter in the milk, then add four cups of dark brown sugar, cook till nearly thick enough to pull like candy, stirring all the time. Let it cool before putting on the cake.

Chocolate Icing.

One cup of milk, one cup of powdered sugar, one-fourth pound of chocolate, (Baker's), one teaspoonful of Gillett's double extract vanilla; scald the milk and chocolate, then add the sugar and pour it on the well-beaten white of an egg, beating constantly for about five minutes.

Macaroon Frosting.

Half pound chopped almonds, not blanched, whites of two eggs, a small cup powdered sugar. Stir the almonds in the eggs and sugar, and spread on top of cake before baking.

ICES, SHERBETS AND ICE CREAMS.

Sherbet.

One quart milk boiled with one pound white sugar and the rind of one lemon, half freeze like snow, then add the juice of six lemons and the whites of five eggs beaten to a stiff froth, freeze hard.

Strawberry Sherbet.

Crush a pound of picked strawberries into a basin, and add a quart of water, with a sliced lemon, and let it stand for two or three hours; put one and one-fourth pounds of sugar into another basin, cover the basin with a cloth, and through this cloth strain the strawberry juice; when the sugar is fully dissolved, strain again, and set the vessel into which it is strained on ice until ready to serve.

Orange Sherbet.

One tablespoonful gelatine, two tablespoonfuls cold water, two large oranges, two lemons, one pint water, half cup of this water boiling hot, to soak gelatine, one and one-half cups sugar. After packing freezer, and dissolving gelatine, put all together and strain into the freezer.

Orange Sherbet.

Juice of six oranges and four lemons, one and one-half pints sugar, one and one-half pints water, one and one-half tablespoonfuls gelatine. For every pint water take one pint sugar, one tablespoonful gelatine; boil the sugar and water and skim, add to it the gelatine, previously soaked in cold water for half an hour; when cool add juice of oranges and lemons, and freeze. Sufficient for eleven persons, and if oranges are juicy, enough for sixteen.

Pine-Apple Sherbet.

Two cans of pine-apple or the same amount of fresh fruit, two pounds of sugar, two quarts water, whites of six eggs, strain juice from the cans into the freezer, make a boiling syrup of the sugar and one quart water, chop the pine-apple small, scald it in the boiling syrup, then rub it through a colander, with the syrup and remaining quart of water, into the freezer; freeze and add the whites of four eggs, and beat it perfectly white.

Bisque.

One pint thick cream, yolks of four eggs, quarter pound of fine sugar, Gillett's double extract vanilla; mix lightly, pack in ice and salt, and let stand three or four hours without stirring.

Lemon Ice.

Put one and one-fourth pounds sugar and a quart of water on to boil, grate the rind of four lemons and one orange, and add to the syrup; when cool add the juice of the lemon and orange, strain all through a cloth, and turn into the freezer; freeze hard.

Orange Ice.

Boil one pound of sugar in a quart of water, when cool add the juice of six oranges, steep the rinds in a little water, strain and use to flavor with if desired. The juice of two lemons added to this is a great improvement. Freeze same as ice cream.

Pine-apple Ice.

One quart can of pine-apple, two pounds of sugar, one quart of water, and the juice of three lemons. Chop the pine-apple very fine, add the sugar, lemon juice and water, then freeze. Serves about ten persons.

Peach Ice.

Three pints of water, two and one-half pounds of sugar; put on stove and let boil clear, put in little white of egg to clarify, skim, let cool, then add can of peaches put through strainer (but do not put in all the pulp), juice and about half the pulp. Add juice of three lemons and freeze. When nearly frozen add well-beaten whites of two eggs and four spoonfuls of sugar. Plenty for twenty-five people if served in cups.

Cranberry Ice.

Four quarts water, two pounds sugar, two quarts cranberries. Boil water and sugar, and skim; stew the berries in a very little water, rub through a sieve and add to the syrup; when cold, freeze.

Raspberry Ice.

One quart of red raspberries, one quart of water, one and one-fourth pounds of sugar, juice of three lemons; mix the sugar with the berries, then add the water and lemon juice, mash fine through a sieve, and turn into a freezer. When frozen will serve seven people.

Strawberry Ice.

Is made same as raspberry.

Coffee Ice.

To one quart of water add one and one-fourth pound sugar; one pint of rich coffee, and freeze.

Roman Punch.

Three cups sugar, two quarts water, juice of two lemons and two oranges brought to a boiling point, three tablespoonfuls rum, and two cups whipped cream, add when partly frozen.

Ice Cream.

One quart of cream, three-fourths cup sugar, one teaspoonful Gillett's double extract of vanilla; whip cream and all together, and freeze.

Chocolate Ice Cream.

One quart of cream, four ounces of chocolate, one tablespoonful of Gillett's extract of vanilla, two large cups of sugar, cinnamon to taste. Cook the cream, chocolate, sugar and vanilla, strain through a sieve, pour into the freezer and let stand two hours.

Banana Ice Cream.

Mash six large bananas in a Keystone egg-beater, one quart cream, two cups of sugar. Cook cream and sugar, when cool add the bananas beaten to a paste, turn into the freezer for two hours.

Apricot Ice Cream.

Apricot cream may be made the same as banana cream.

Strawberry Ice Cream.

Strawberry ice cream may be made the same as banana cream.

Raspberry Ice Cream.

Raspberry ice cream may be made the same as banana cream.

Vanilla Ice Cream.

One pint of milk thickened in farina boiler with one teaspoonful flour, three eggs, and one cup of sugar; strain, and when cool add two quarts of cream and one cup of sugar; season to taste with Gillett's double extract of vanilla; freeze.

Lemon Ice Cream.

One quart of cream, one-half pound of sugar. juice and grated rind of two lemons and one orange, When the cream has been heated set away to cool; mix the sugar with the lemons and orange, then set it away to cool. Put the cream in the freezer, when partially frozen add the lemons, etc., and set away.

Peach Ice Cream.

One quart of soft, ripe peaches, mashed fine, one pint of cream, one pint of milk, with half an ounce of gelatine dissolved in it, one pound sugar; turn into a freezer.

Peach Ice Cream, No. 2.

One pint cream, one pint mashed peaches, one glass milk, one to two teacupfuls sugar. Freeze.

Fruit Ice Cream.

One quart of milk, one ounce of gelatine dissolved in the milk, three eggs well-beaten, and one pound of sugar. When partially frozen add one cup of strawberries, one cup of chopped raisins, one cup of chopped almonds, part of a cocoanut grated, and a cup of currants. Freeze.

Fig Cream.

Four quarts cream, one and one-half pounds sugar, two pounds figs chopped fine, four tablespoonfuls Gillett's double extract vanilla. Scald half the cream with the sugar, add the rest when cold, and add figs when mixture is partly frozen. Enough for thirty-two people.

Coffee Ice Cream.

Three quarts pure cream, one pint *strong* coffee, one and one-half pounds sugar. Scald half the cream with the sugar, when cold add to the cold cream, add coffee and freeze.

Orange Souffle.

To a quart of cream allow a pint of orange juice, yolks of six eggs, one pound of sugar and one-half box of gelatine. Soak gelatine one hour in a cup of cold water, then add one-half cup of boiling water; mix orange juice, sugar and whipped cream; beat yolks of eggs until light, add juice, sugar and cream, stir in gelatine, strain, freeze and let stand. This is very rich but nice for a change.

Tutti Frutti.

Two quarts of orange ice, one pound candied cherries, one pound candied pine-apple, one pound chopped almonds, one pound candied apricots. Chop fruit very fine, after the ice is well frozen, stir the chopped fruit in and stir thoroughly, then stand away for three hours.

CANDIES.

Peanut Candy.

Melt two cups granulated sugar by heat, adding one cup shelled peanuts when nearly done, pour out on buttered plates and let cool.

Cocoanut Cream Candy.

Three cups white sugar, scant half cup of water, half teaspoonful cream tartar; boil ten minutes, then add one cup of fresh cocoanut or desicated; beat well together and drop on white paper by the spoonful.

Chocolate Creams.

Two cups pulverized sugar, half cup cream, boil five minutes or until it is hard enough to mold when dropped in cold water; then stir until cool enough to make into balls; grate the chocolate and steam over a tea-kettle; when soft, cover the balls by dipping them in on a fork, set in a cool place

Chocolate Cream Drops.

Mix half a teacupful cream with two cups of white sugar, boil and stir for five minutes; set the dish into another one of cold water, and stir the syrup until it becomes hard, then make into small balls, about the size of a marble, with a fork roll each one separately in the chocolate, (three-fourths of a cake of chocolate melted). Put on brown paper to cool; half tablespoonful Gillett's double extract of vanilla may be added to the cream if desired.

English Walnut Candy.

One pound of confectionery sugar, white of one egg, as much water as the white; pour in sugar until thick enough to handle; when ready, put on bread board and knead fifteen minutes; roll out smooth and cut into squares; have a pound of English walnuts broken in halves and place between.

Caramels.

One cake Baker s chocolate, four cups of brown sugar, quarter pound of butter, large cup of milk, boil until it will harden slightly in cold water, beat and add one tablespoonful of Gillett's double extract of vanilla and white of one egg; put into pans and cut into squares when cold.

Chocolate Caramels.

Three pounds of brown sugar, half pound of butter, one cake of Baker's chocolate, three gills of milk, one tablespoonful of Gillett's double extract vanilla.

Maple Caramels.

Melt one pound maple sugar in a cup of sweet milk and one tablespoonful butter; soak until almost brittle, turn on a buttered platter, when cool enough mark in squares.

Marsh Mallows.

Dissolve half a pound white gum arabic in one pint of water, strain and add half pound fine sugar, place over the fire, stirring constantly until the sugar is dissolved, and all is the consistency of honey; add gradually the whites of four eggs well-beaten, stir the mixture until it becomes somewhat thick and does not adhere to the finger; pour into a tin slightly powdered with starch, and when cool divide off into squares.

Molasses Taffy.

One cup sugar, one cup molasses, one large tablespoonful butter, three tablespoonfuls vinegar.

Molasses Candy.

Two cups N. O. molasses, one cup white sugar, butter half the size of an egg, two teaspoonfuls vinegar; boil until candy hardens in cold water.

Butter Scotch.

Three tablespoonfuls of molasses, two tablespoonfuls of sugar, two tablespoonfuls of water, one tablespoonful of butter; add a pinch of soda before taking up.

Cream Candy.

One pound white sugar, one wine glass vinegar, one tumbler water, Gillett's double extract vanilla; boil half hour and pull if you choose.

Salted Almonds.

Blanch the almonds, and spread out to dry for several hours; put a good sized piece of butter into a dripping pan, and as it warms stir the almonds over and over to coat them with butter; set in the oven, stirring often, until they begin to color faintly, shake in colander to rid of grease, spread on a dish and sprinkle with salt, stirring them about so that each meat may have its share, and avoid getting them too brown.

BEVERAGES.

Chocolate.

Five tablespoonfuls of scraped chocolate, one quart of milk, one quart of boiling water, two tablespoonfuls of sugar. Dissolve the chocolate in a little boiling water, set the milk and water over the fire and as soon as it comes to a boil put in the dissolved chocolate and add the sugar, boil a few minutes and it is ready to serve. This amount of sugar may be too much for some people; less is required for sweet choclate.

Cocoa and Cocoa Nibs are made in the same way. It should always be served *hot*, a little cold milk is often added at the table. This is a very healthful drink; it is good for children and nervous people. It is also nutritious and exhilarating.

Chocolate, No. 2.

Two ounces chocolate shaved fine and put in a saucepan with two tablespoonfuls boiling water, add half a pint boiling water, two tablespoonfuls sugar, a pinch of salt, one tablespoonful cornstarch, dissolved, boil five minutes. When ready to serve add one pint boiling milk and let boil up once, serve with whipped cream. This makes six cups and can be made the day before you wish to use it.

Russian Tea.

Pare and slice good juicy lemons and lay a piece in the bottom of each cup, sprinkle with white sugar and pour hot strong tea upon it. Do not use cream.

Lime Water.

This is easily made at home by taking a piece of unslacked lime the size of a walnut, and putting it into two quarts of filtered water in an earthern vessel and stirring it thoroughly; allow it to settle and pour off the clear solution as required for use, replacing with water and stirring up as consumed. This is useful in certain acid conditions of the stomach, and is often called for in treating infants.

Sweet Whey.

To a pint of milk add about a square inch of rennet and slowly warm to about one hundred degrees Fahr., stand for thirty minutes and then strain through muslin.

Grape Juice.

To every five pounds of grapes, one pound of sugar and one quart of hot water; let it just come to a boil, put through a crash towel bag; take pulp that remains in bag, put in a dish and put one quart water to wash all juice, then drain in bag and add sugar, water and juice, put on stove, let come to a boil, and seal in glass jars while hot.

Strawberry Wine.

To the juice of three quarts of strawberries mashed and strained, add half the quantity of red currant juice. Put to each quart of fruit juice one quart of water and one pound of loaf sugar; ferment it in a clean, sweet cask, leaving the bung out; when fermentation has ceased, put into bottles and cork it for use. It is a very pleasant wine for invalids, and also for cooking purposes.

Milk Punch.

One tumbler of milk well sweetened, two tablespoonfuls brandy well stirred in. Serve very cold with ice.

Koumiss. (Sometimes called Sour Beer.)

Into one quart of new milk put one gill of fresh buttermilk and three or four lumps of white sugar; mix well, and see that the sugar dissolves. Put in warm place to stand ten hours when it will be thick. Pour from one vessel to another until it becomes smooth and uniform in consistency. Bottle and keep in warm place twenty-four hours, it may take thirty-six in winter. The bottles must be tightly corked, and the corks tied down. Shake well five minutes before opening. It makes a very agreeable drink, which is especially recommended for persons who do not assimilate their food, and for young children; may be drank as freely as milk. Instead of buttermilk some use a teaspoonful of yeast. The richer your milk, which should be unskimmed, the better will be your Koumiss.

Blackberry Cordial.

Secure ripe berries and crush them, to each gallon of juice add one quart of boiling water, let it stand twenty-four hours, stirring it a few times; strain and add two pounds of sugar to each gallon of liquid; put in jugs and cork tightly. It may be used in two months, is excellent for summer complaint, and can be taken by delicate invalids.

Currant Wine.

One quart of currant juice to three pounds of sugar, with sufficient water added to make gallon.

Raspberry Shrub.

Four quarts of red raspberries to one of vinegar, let stand four days then strain; to each pint of juice add a pound of sugar. Boil twenty minutes; bottle and keep in a dry, cool place.

Rice Water.

Wash well one ounce of the best rice in cold water, then soak for three hours in a quart of water kept at a tepid heat; then boil slowly for one hour and strain. This may be flavored with cloves or other spices.

Arrowroot.

Mix two tablespoonfuls arrowroot with three tablespoonfuls cold water; add half a pint of boiling water, constantly stirring, (milk may be added in stead of water); flavor with sugar, nutmeg or other spice. This preparation is suitable when the bowels are inflamed and relaxed.

Egg Nogg.

Six eggs well-beaten (whites and yolks separately), one quart milk, half cup sugar, half pint brandy, nutmeg. Stir yolks into the milk, with the sugar first beaten into the yolks; add brandy, then whites of eggs; whip well.

Egg Nogg, No. 2.

Scald some new milk by putting it (contained in a new fruit jar with screw cover) into a sauce pan of boiling water, *but it must not be allowed to boil*; beat ap a fresh egg with a fork in a tumbler, with some sugar, beat to a froth; then add a dessert spoonful of brandy or port wine, and fill up the tumbler with scalded milk when cold. This is a highly nutritious diet suitable at the begining of convalescence after severe acute illness.

Egg Nogg, No. 3.

One egg, one teaspoonful sugar, one tablespoonful whisky, one-third glass milk, a little nutmeg, and a piece of ice the size of a walnut. Beat the yolk of egg, sugar and whisky together, beat the white of egg very stiff; mix; put in and fill glass with milk, grate the nutmeg on top.

Egg Lemonade.

This is a refreshing and nutritious drink, especially for invalids. A tin shaker and a small wooden pestle are necessary. Put half of a large lemon in a glass, after extracting the seeds, also three lumps of sugar, press and work with the pestle till the juice is extracted and the skin soft· add two tablespoonfuls of sugar, the same of finely cracked ice, and one raw egg, fill nearly full with cold water, invert the tin shaker over it and shake well. This is not so good without the ice, and should be cracked very fine. Put two straws in the glass and serve.

Lemonade.

Four medium sized lemons, three pints of water, sugar to taste. Cut the lemons in two after washing them thoroughly; place one-half at a time in a lemon squeezer and squeeze dry; put the juice in a pitcher with the sugar and pour on the water, add the ice in small pieces, when dissolved stir and serve.

Acid Lemonade.

One lemon, one teaspoonful tartaric acid, one teaspoonful of Gillett's lemon extract, three pints of water, sugar to taste. Squeeze the lemon in a lemon squeezer, dissolve the acid, put the lemon juice, acid, sugar and lemon extract in a pitcher, mix thoroughly and pour on the water, add ice. If a strong ade is desired use only a quart of water. Put the rind of the lemon in the pitcher.

Lime Ade.

Lime ade is made the same as above; a little more sugar is needed than for lemons. This is very refreshing and preferable to lemonade in the summer.

Orange Ade.

Four or five sour oranges, sugar, ice-water; make as you would lemonade.

Tea.

Colored teas are injurious and should not be used. Black tea, or uncolored Japan, if of a good quality are free from the coloring matter often used in teas. Green tea is dried on copper plates and therefore is unwholesome. Strong decoctions of tea are bad for nervous people and harmful for nearly every one.

To Make Tea.

Scald the tea steeper, put in a small teaspoonful for each person, pour boiling water over it and steep for four or five minutes. Pour boiling water in the tea-pot to heat it, when the tea is steeped pour the water from the tea-pot, put in the tea and fill up with boiling water. Another way is to make the tea at the table; heat the china or silver tea-pot by filling with water, pour it out, put in the tea and boiling water; when it has stood a few minutes it is ready to serve.

Coffee.

Allow a dessert spoonful to each person and one for the coffee-pot; put the coffee in the bowl with the white of an egg and a little cold water, stir all together thoroughly, then put it in the coffee-pot, pour boiling water over it and place on the stove; cover the spout of the coffee-pot to preserve the aroma; as soon as it boils up set it on the back of the stove to steep and settle. Coffee made in this way is delicious with cream and sugar. Every kind of coffee can be made as above. Old Government Java and Mocha are good coffees and have a fine flavor, they are very often mixed and the flavor is better than when used separately, two-thirds Java and one-third Mocha is the proportion used of each. In serving coffee pour it over the cream and sugar in the cups. If milk is used heat it and add a beaten egg, as the two combined make a good substitute for cream.

After Dinner Coffee.

Make as above only have it very strong and black. Serve in small china cups and fill them only half full, pass sugar and cream with the coffee.

To Roast Coffee.

Wash the coffee in warm water, drain through a colander and dry on a towel, then put it in a dripping pan and brown in the oven; do not allow it to burn, stir often that it may be evenly browned, it should be of a dark brown color; when done put a small piece of butter with it and stir the coffee. Keep coffee in a caddy or tightly closed dish. Grind only enough for each meal at a time, as the aroma escapes from ground coffee.

ODDS AND ENDS.

Strawberry Jam.

Three-fourths pound sugar to one of fruit; mash the fruit and sugar together and boil.

Baking Powder Biscuits.

Three teaspoonfuls Gillett's cream tartar baking powder, half teaspoonful salt, two heaping tablespoonfuls butter to a quart of flour if milk is used, if water is used four tablespoonfuls will be required.

First sift baking powder well through the flour, add salt, work butter thoroughly, then mix lightly and quickly with milk or water into a soft dough.

Grape Jam.

Separate the skins from the pulp, keeping in separate dishes, put the pulps in kettle, with a teacupful of water, when thoroughly heated run through a colander to separate the seeds. Then put your skins with pulp and weigh; to each pound of fruit put three-fourths pound sugar, add merely water enough to keep from burning; cook slowly three-fourths of an hour, or till thick enough.

Fruit Gelatine.

One-third of an ounce package of gelatine to one pint of liquid, juice of two lemons and two oranges, soak gelatine a few minutes in a half cup of cold water, then half a cup of hot water; add the lemon and orange juice, and if not enough liquid to make a pint add more water, sweeten to taste, strain all through a fine strainer, put in a cool place and as soon as it begins to set, put a layer of jelly in your mold, then a layer of sliced bananas, or candied cherries (or other fruits), a layer of jelly, and so on until all is used; put in ice box until firm enough to turn out.

Fruit Salad.

Soak half a box of gelatine in a little water on the back of the stove, use fresh fruits in season and canned fruits, (use two or more kinds), put a layer of one kind in your mold, cover with sugar, another kind and sugar, ctc., put the fruit from the canned fruit in in a dish, cover the mold tightly with a plate, turn over and drain the juice into the dish of liquor, mix the liquor and gelatine thoroughly, then pour over the fruit, put in the ice box to cool. Two kinds of fruit may be used, but a different fruit for each layer makes a prettier dish.

Breakfast Buns.

One egg beaten separately, to the yolk add one teaspoonful sugar and stir thoroughly, to this add one-fourth cup butter, half cup sweet milk; one pint sifted flour. Mix very lightly, add one teaspoonful Gillett's cream tartar baking powder, then last drop the white of the egg, beaten stiff, over the mixture, and add trifle more flour; stir, and empty onto a floured molding board, roll out half inch thick and grease surface with melted butter; cut with large biscuit cutter and fold like turnover. Bake in hot oven after breakfast is ready to serve.

Brown Bread.

One cup sour milk, two cups sweet milk, one cup molasses, one cup of wheat flour, one cup Graham flour, two cups Indian meal, one teaspoonful soda, one teaspoonful salt, steam three hours.

Hermits.

One and one-half cups sugar, one cup melted butter, one cup chopped raisins, three eggs, one teaspoonful each of cloves, allspice, cinnamon and lemon juice, one teaspoonful soda dissolved in four tablespoonfuls cold water; mix stiff and roll thin.

Snow Pudding.

Bake six medium-sized sour apples, whites of two eggs, one cup of white sugar; beat the pulp, sugar and eggs together; serve with cream.

Graham Pudding.

Half cup sugar, half cup molasses, one cup sour milk, two and one-half cups of Graham flour, one cup raisins, one teaspoonful soda; steam one hour.

SAUCE.—Two-thirds cup sugar, one cup water, small piece butter, juice of half a lemon.

Cookies.

One cup butter, two cups sugar, one cup sweet milk' one egg, half teaspoonful soda, one tablespoonful cream tartar, flour to roll thin.

Sole.

Take the fillets of sole, role up size of large cork, place in pan, moisten with Rhine wine, cover and steam in oven until well cooked, dish fillets, add little more wine to pan, small piece of butter and salt; add yolks of six eggs, whip to a yellow foam, and pour over the fish.

Souffle for Soup.

Mix one-half ounce flour with a llttle boiling water, salt, remove from fire, add two eggs, roll thin, cut in strips, form them into small pills, roll around in sieve, fry in hot lard, serve on top of the soup.

Brouchee Salpicon.

Make very small patties of puff paste, or fry a batter on iron form, drop off, for the salpicon cases. Make a salpicon of the following ingredients, all well cooked the day before, cut in small dice, a tablespoonful each of sweetbreads, red tongue, ox palate, mushrooms, chicken liver, rooster comb, lamb fries, lastly one truffle, cut as rest. Put all in small saucepan, add enough brown sauce (Espagnole) and tomato sauce, half and half, to moisten, small piece of glace, one tablespoonful of good sherry wine, let simmer five minutes, fill up the brouchee at the moment of serving.

Golden Cream.

Put small can of pumpkin or the same amount of fresh boiled pumpkin in sauce pan, add a pint of chicken broth, season with nutmeg, red pepper, salt and small piece of butter, let it come to a boil, remove from the fire, add one quart of pure cream sauce made thin and pass all through a fine strainer. Serve very hot; do not boil.

Vanilla Souffle.

Boil half a pint of milk in a farina boiler, then mix five tablespoonfuls flour with another half pint of cold milk until it is smooth, then add gradually to the boiling milk, stiring constantly until thick. Beat the yolks of five eggs and two tablespoonfuls sugar together until very light and add them to the flour mixture. Then beat the whites of the eggs stiff and beat them into the mixture, and add one teaspoonful Gillett's double extract vanilla; butter a pudding mold, put some dried cherries or raisins in the bottom, pour in the mixture, cover and tie it, and boil in a kettle of water one and a half hours, remove the lid and allow the pudding to stand a few minutes before turning out; serve with a liquid pudding sauce.

Custard Souffle.

Boil half a pint of milk in a double boiler, rub two tablespoonfuls flour, and two of butter together until smooth, then add to the milk till it thickens; beat the yolks of four eggs and two tablespoonfuls of sugar together and add them to the hot milk, then set to cool; when thoroughly cold add the well beaten whites of the eggs to the mixture, mix well, tnrn into a greased dish and bake quickly for twenty minutes; to be served at once with a foamy sauce.

Wafer Pudding.

Put half a pint of milk in a double boiler, when boiling hot add a quarter pound of butter, stir until dissolved, then throw in two ounces of flour and stir quickly until thick and smooth, take from the fire and let cool; beat four eggs very light and add to the mixture, beat all rapidly a few minutes; grease gem pans and put a tablespoonful of this mixture in each one, and bake in a quick oven about forty minutes; serve with foamy sauce.

Macaroni Pudding.

Half pound of macaroni boiled twenty minutes, put it on in boiling water with a dessertspoonful salt, when cooked strain through a sieve and let plenty of cold water run over it to prevent sticking. Beat four eggs, and pour over it one pint milk and four tablespoonfuls sugar, a good tablespoonful butter, mix well, and bake brown.

Spanish Bun Cake.

One whole egg, the yolks of three, two cups sugar, half cup butter, one cup milk, two cups flour, two teaspoonfuls Gillett's cream tartar baking powder, one heaping dessertspoonful spice; make frosting with the other whites.

Orange Marmalade.

Nine Seville oranges, three sweet oranges, three lemons; cut the fruit across the grain in the finest possible slices, lay them in three quarts of cold water for thirty-six hours or more, then boil quickly for two hours, after which add eight pounds of white sugar, and boil for another hour or until it jellies.

Cocoa Bon-bons.

Into the white of one egg and an equal quantity of water, stir enough cocoanut pulverized to enable you to roll it into balls; boil until it creams, two cups sugar, one cup water, stirring constantly; when it creams, flavor with Gillett's double extract vanilla, and roll the cocoanut balls in it as you would chocolate creams. Set the cream dish in a dish of boiling water and it will not harden too soon.

Albany Rolls.

One pint milk, let it boil, put in butter the size of an egg, let it cool, add one teaspoonful sugar and pinch of salt, stir in with a spoon as much flour as possible, add half cup of water, let rise over night, take small pieces, knead them, let rise again and bake.

Cocoanut Jelly Cake.

Half cup butter, one cup sugar, half cup milk, two eggs, two and one-half cups flour, two heaping teaspoonfuls Gillett's cream tartar baking powder.

FILLING.—After heating half cup milk, add one teaspoonful cornstarch dissolved in a little cold milk, one tablespoonful sugar, yolk of one egg, and cocoanut to taste.

Cream Nectar.

Two ounces tartaric acid, two and one-half pounds white sugar, the juice of half a lemon, three pints of water; boil all together five minutes, when nearly cold add the whites of three eggs well-beaten with half cup of flour, one ounce of Gillett's essence wintergreen, bottle and keep in a cool place, take one spoonful of this to a glass of water, add half teaspoonful soda and stir.

Pickelette.

Four large cabbages chopped fine, one quart onions chopped fine, two quarts vinegar, two pounds brown sugar, two tablespoonfuls ground mustard, and black pepper, cinnamon, turmeric, celery seed, one tablespoonful allspice, mace, pulverized alum, pack the cabbage and onions in alternate layers with a little salt between them, let stand twenty-four hours, then scald the vinegar and spices together, pour on the cabbage and onions after draining; do this for three mornings, heat to a scald, let boil five minutes, when cold pack in small jars.

Chocolate Frosted Cake.

Yolks four eggs, one whole egg, (beat the whites separately), one cup sugar, half cup sweet milk, one tablespoonful butter, one and one-half cups flour, one and one-half teaspoonfuls of Gillett's cream tartar baking powder, flavor with Gillett's double extract vanilla.

Frosting.—One cup sugar, white of one egg, one square chocolate, cut it and melt in dish, and add to frosting after 'tis beaten, flavor with Gillett's double extract vanilla.

Graham Gems.

Three eggs beaten till light, small tablespoonful melted butter, one and one-half cups sweet milk, one pint of Graham flour, one and one-half teaspoonfuls Gillett's cream tartar baking powder, pinch of salt; have muffin tins *very hot;* bake fifteen minutes.

Cabbage Pickles.

Slice very fine the best part of two heads of cabbage, chop fine six green tomatoes, sprinkle with salt, lay over night, drain in the morning, add six green peppers chopped fine, one-fourth pound each of white and black mustard seed, a bowl of grated horseradish, ground cinnamon to taste. Put together in a jar, add two pounds light brown sugar, mix thoroughly and cover with cold vinegar.

Hollandaise Potatoes.

With French potato cutter, cut out round potato balls, boil in salt water just done, drain, dish, pour over chopped parsley with melted butter.

Mikado Ice Cream.

Fill little mikado molds with ice cream, place in freezer until wanted, turn out, place a Japanese umbrella in the arm of each, and serve at once.

Raspberry Fritters.

Put one cup of flour into a bowl, then add the well beaten yolks of three eggs and a gill of cold water. beat till all is very light, add one teaspoonful salt; Beat one pint of raspberries with an egg beater until thoroughly broken, then beat the whites of two eggs to a stiff froth, add them to the batter, then add the fruit and one teaspoonful Gillett's cream tartar baking powder. Have ready your hot lard, drop a spoonful at a time, drain on brown paper, and dredge with powdered sugar,

Strawberry Pancakes.

Whip one pint of strawberries with an egg beater until smooth, then beat the whites of three eggs, add to them two tablespoonfuls of powdered sugar and beat again until the eggs are fine and stiff, add the yolks, then the strawberry juice, mix carefully, add one cup of sifted flour with one teaspoonful Gillett's cream tartar baking powder in it. Bake on a griddle, serve very hot with powdered sugar. Very delicious for dessert.

HOW

to Remove Mildew from Linen.

Take your clothes when dry and wet thoroughly with soft soap and salt mixed, chalk or starch scraped to a powder may be used instead of salt. Lay out to bleach on the grass. If once does not do, use the second time and the linen will be as clean and clear as ever.

to make Chewing Gum.

Prepared balsam of tulu two ounces, refined sugar one ounce, oatmeal three ounces; soak the gum in water, then mix all the ingredients, roll in powdered sugar to make the sticks.

to make Caramel.

Boil clarified sugar until it is very brittle, pour on an oiled slab, soon as cool enough to receive an impression from the finger, stamping it in small squares an inch in size, then turning over the mass, wiping the bottom and putting in a dry place to harden. Glaze with a coating of sugar and keep from the air.

to make Colorings for Confectionery.

The following coloring matters are admitted to be harmless.

For YELLOW.—Use Persian fustic, turmeric or saffron.

For BLUES.—Use ultramarine, indigo, Prussian blue.

For REDS.—Use carmine, cochineal.

For Greens.—It is best to blend any of the above blues and yellow together, a little practice will enable you to hit upon the exact tint that you want.

For Purple.—Mix blue and red in proportions to yield the exact color wanted.

For Browns.—Chocolate or burnt caramels will produce nearly every shade of brown as they are more or less weakened by water.

to make Butter.

Warm your cream to a temperature of 58° to 63°, Fahr.; a comparatively slow motion is the best, a forward and backward movement, one revolution each way, keeps the cream at the bottom of the churn. After the butter comes, pour off the buttermilk, then beat awhile longer with the whips, this works it sufficient for immediate use. But for preserving it should be worked a little more with the paddle, adding two even teaspoonfuls of very fine salt to each pound of butter. To wash butter deprives it of part of its preserving qualities.

To take Stains out of White Goods.

One teaspoonful chloride of lime in about three quarts of water; put the part that is stained in the water, and let remain until the stain is out.

To Prepare Fruit for Canning.

The following table, giving the length of time for boiling fruit and the right proportion of sugar to the quart of fruit to be used, will be of value to housewives in canning fruit time:

	Minutes.	Sugar, ozs.
Cherries,	5	8
Raspberries,	6	8
Blackberries,	8	8
Strawberries,	8	8
Whortleberries,	5	6
Plums,	10	8
Pie Plant (sliced),	10	10
Small Pears (whole),	30	6
Bartlett Pears (in halves),	20	8
Peaches (whole),	15	6
Peaches (in halves),	8	6
Pineapple (sliced),	15	8
Siberian crabapple (whole),	25	10
Sour apple (quartered),	10	8
Ripe currants,	6	10
Grapes (sweet),	10	8
Grapes (sour),	10	10

Place the fruit in glass cans. Make a syrup of the required amount of sugar, putting in as little water as possible for the number of cans to be filled. After the syrup cools a little pour into the cans, filling them nearly full; if there is not enough syrup add water and place covers on without sealing. Then put the cans in a kettle of cold or warm water having some nails or other hard substance in the bottom. Be careful not to let water boil into the cans. Boil the required time. After taking from the boiling water fill with hot syrup if there is any left or use hot water. Seal, place on the side and turn the can a moment; this allows the air to escape. Fill again and seal.

Breakfast.

Cantalopes,
Oat Flakes with Cream,
Fried Whitefish, Ham Omelet,
Duchesse Potatoes,
Rice Waffles, Coffee.

Breakfast, No. 2.

Strawberries and Cream,
Wheat Granules with Cream and Sugar,
Broiled Spring Chicken, Boiled Eggs,
Potatoes Hashed and Browned,
Popovers, Corn Oysters, Coffee.

Breakfast, No. 3.

Oranges,
Oatmeal with Cream and Sugar.
Broiled Mutton Chops, Plain Omelet,
Potatoes cooked in Cream,
White Gems, Coffee.

Breakfast, No. 4.

Bananas and Oranges,
Hominy with Cream and Sugar,
Bacon and Eggs, French Fried Potatoes,
Corn Bread, Coffee.

Lunch.

Individual Scalloped Oysters,
Croquettes of Sweetbreads, Duchesse Potatoes,
Chicken Salad,
Strawberries and Cream, Angel Food Cake,
Coffee.

Lunch, No. 2.

Fried Chicken, Potatoes in Cream,
Mayonnaise of Salmon, Cheese Straws,
Peach Ice Cream, Assorted Cake,
Coffee, Chocolate.

Lunch, No. 3.

Broiled Lamb Chops with Green Peas,
Parkerhouse Rolls, Tomato Salad,
Banana Fritters with Maple Syrup,
Wafers, Chocolate.

Lunch, No. 4.

Fried Oysters, Stuffed Potatoes,
Salmon Salad,
Hot Rolls, Lemon Jelly with Custard,
Small Cakes, Coffee.

Dinner.

Tomato soup with croutons,
Roast Turkey with Giblet Sauce,
Cranberries,
Corn Oysters, French Peas,
Roman Punch,
Broiled Woodcock, Baked Macaroni and Cheese,
Lettuce Salad with Mayonnaise,
English Plum Pudding, Brandy Sauce,
Crackers, Cheese,
Coffee.

Dinner, No. 2.

Puree of Tomato,
Baked Black Bass with Cream Sauce,
Boiled Leg of Mutton with Caper Sauce,
String Beans, Peas,
Lettuce with French Dressing,
Wafers, Cheese,
Caramel Pudding,
Coffee.

Dinner, No. 3.

Cream of Celery,
Ribs of Beef with Yorkshire Pudding,
Squash, Corn Oysters,
Water Cress Salad, Cheese Straws,
Crackers, Cream Cheese,
Frozen Pudding,
Coffee.

Dinner, No. 4.

Cream of Asparagus Soup,
Baked White Fish with Egg Sauce,
Fillet of Beef larded, Mushrooms, Scalloped Potatoes
Peas, Browned Parsnips,
Tomato and Lettuce Salad with French Dressing,
Bent's Water Crackers, Neufchatel Cheese,
New York Ice Cream,
Coffee.

A Country Wedding Feast.

A great long table fairly crammed
With boils and bakes, with stews and steaks,
   With roasts and pies, and stomach aches
Of ever fashion and every size,
   From doughnuts up to pumpkin pies;
With candies, oranges and figs,
   And raisins, and all the whirligigs,
And jimcracks that the law allows
   On such occasions, bobs and buns
Of giggling girls with glossy curls,
   And fancy ribbons, red and blue,
With beau-catchers and curlycues
   To beat the world.
                          —*James Whitcomb Riley.*

FLAVORING EXTRACTS

Are a luxury and appreciated only by those who judge them by their delicacy and strength of flavor. Of the thousands of cheap brands we care not to talk. They are without exception either rank in flavor or weak and expensive at any cost.

Dealers handle them only because they yield a large profit. The best grades are in all respects the cheapest. They go farther and tickle the palate with the deliciousness they impart to the food.

Of all the well-known brands none excel, few if any equal

GILLETT'S DOUBLE EXTRACTS

Over Forty Years in the Market. If your grocer don't sell them, write to the publisher of this book.

www.ingramcontent.com/pod-product-compliance
Lightning Source LLC
Chambersburg PA
CBHW032105230426
43672CB00009B/1649